ANK-INDUSTRY NETWORKS AND CONOMIC EVOLUTION

Bank-Industry Networks and Economic Evolution

An institutional-evolutionary approach

THOMAS MARMEFELT
Jönköping International Business School

Ashgate
Aldershot · Brookfield USA · Singapore · Sydney

Published by
Ashgate Publishing Ltd
Gower House
Croft Road
Aldershot
Hants GU11 3HR
England

Ashgate Publishing Company
Old Post Road
Brookfield
Vermont 05036
USA

British Library Cataloguing in Publication Data
Marmefelt, Thomas
Bank-industry networks and economic evolution : an institutional-evolutionary approach
1. Banks and banking 2. Economic development 3. Industries
I. Title
332.1

Library of Congress Catalog Card Number: 98-71397

ISBN 1 84014 574 9

Printed and bound by Athenaeum Press, Ltd.,
Gateshead, Tyne & Wear.

Contents

Preface

This book presents an outline of an institutional-evolutionary theory of institutional change, innovation, and financial systems, based on learning-by-financing within bank-industry networks.

Innovation leads to economic growth through a qualitative improvement of the economic process called economic evolution. Yet, innovation is more than technological change. The financial and institutional dimensions are important, but often neglected, aspects of the innovation process.

Joseph Schumpeter recognized that credit is crucial to innovation, thus establishing a theoretical link between finance and economic evolution. As innovation is characterized by uncertainty and bounded rationality, the institutional forms of interaction between bankers and entrepreneurs become most important. The evolution of the securitized economy has often been associated with financial disintermediation. Rejecting that this would be a necessary outcome, I develop a set of models in order to outline a theoretical explanation why the bank-industry network around a universal bank is viable as institutional form for industrial banking and the financing of innovation in a securitized economy.

A preliminary version was written when I was at the Ecole des Hautes Etudes en Sciences Sociales. Later I made revisions at the Jönköping International Business School. This book is based on my own ideas, but I would like to acknowledge some individuals for constructive comments. The following individuals have influenced the evolution of my book: Michel Aglietta, Per-Olof Bjuggren, Gunnar Eliasson, Rauf Gönenç, Börje Johansson, Håkan Lindgren, and Ulrich Witt.

During the cumbersome final stage, my girlfriend, Jurgita Baniūnaitė, made me look on the bright side of life.

Finally, I would like to thank my parents, Dan and Ulla Marmefelt, for their continuous encouragement.

Jönköping
February 1998

1 Introduction

1.1 Problem

National systems for financing innovations have recently received attention. OECD (1995) provides a foundation for comparative analysis of the links between innovation and financial systems in the emerging knowledge-based economy. However, there is no comprehensive theory of institutional change, innovation, and financial systems, although Day, Eliasson, and Wihlborg (1993) contribute by bringing the markets for innovation, ownership, and control together. Having Schumpeter's (1911) theory of economic evolution as starting point, my contribution is to give an outline of an institutional-evolutionary theory of institutional change, innovation, and financial systems. Schumpeterian banker-entrepreneur interaction, institutional change, and economic evolution are brought together in a theory based on the learning-by-financing within bank-industry networks, such as Japanese keiretsu groups or Swedish ownership spheres.

Bank-industry networks connecting banks, owners, and industrial firms allow for continuous interaction between bankers and entrepreneurs. Learning-by-financing arises when the interaction give the banker the opportunity to produce private information about the entrepreneur. The information costs involved in the innovation process would thereby decrease, thus facilitating the improvement of the organizational and technological level of the economy, i.e. a quality upgrading of the economic process.

In this book, my purpose is to answer three questions:

(i) How does learning-by-financing within bank-industry networks influence the quality upgrading of the economic process?

(ii) How do bank-industry networks evolve through evolutionary selection as bankers and entrepreneurs interact?

(iii) What conditions are crucial for the evolutionary viability of the universal bank as network bank in a securitized economy?

For this purpose, I will develop a set of models in order to outline a theoretical explanation why the bank-industry network around a universal bank is viable as an institutional form for industrial banking in a securitized economy.

1.2 Relations to the Literature

1.2.1 Innovation and Economic Evolution

Following Schumpeter (1911), credit creation yields innovation which in turn makes the economic process break away from the stationary circular flow into a disequilibrium process. The circular flow is a Walrasian general equilibrium in which there is no economic evolution. Profits and interest streams are zero. Entrepreneurs break the circular flow when they realize new combinations of products, processes, types of organization, sources of supply, and markets. In this way, they improve the quality of the economic process, thus reducing the increase of entropy, as less free energy (resources) is transformed into bounded energy (waste) in the process of producing a given output (Georgescu-Roegen, 1971).[1] As the quality improves, the economy reaches higher levels of economic development. Hence, the disequilibrium process yields transient monopoly profits which are an entrepreneurial rent for the quality upgrading of the economic process and an interest stream to the bankers for their supplying the crucial credit.

While innovation is the disequilibrium force of economic evolution, imitation is the equilibrium force, thus moving the economy to a new circular flow at a higher level of economic development. This differs from Kirzner's (1973) view of entrepreneurship as an equilibrium force, since Schumpeterian entrepreneurs create disequilibrium. Nevertheless, Schumpeterian dynamics give a distribution of efficiencies which remains relatively stable in the long run, all of them being on a higher level (Iwai, 1984a,b). Using Salter's (1960) vintage approach, Iwai's analysis implies that the best practice vintage would, if the long-run distribution of efficiencies is stable, determine the performance levels for all existing vintages in the economy down to the worst practice vintage. The required performance levels for all existing vintages increase through innovation and imitation.

Economic growth, where more inputs are used in the old economic process, differs from economic evolution in Schumpeter's theory, since there is no quality upgrading of the economic process. In von Neumann's (1945) growth model of an expanding economy with a linear technology, where a set of activities transform a number of inputs to the same number of outputs, the equilibrium growth rate equals an interest rate on holding money due to falling prices on all goods. This is consistent with Schumpeter's circular flow, since economic evolution would require that new activities of a higher quality, which transform a given number of inputs to a larger number of outputs than before, continuously enter and over time crowd out the old activities.

In Schumpeter's theory, however, the interest rate is the unit price the entrepreneur pays for buying purchasing power from the banker. According to Schumpeter, credit creation through the banking system is a necessary condition for innovation. The uncertainty of the innovation process and the bounded rationality of economic agents give credit creation and financial institutions a crucial role. The institutional forms for interaction between bankers and entrepreneurs matter.

I consider the efficiency of the financial system as a set of institutions which support innovation and economic evolution. Hence, my focus is what Tobin (1984) would call the functional efficiency of the financial system.

1.2.2 Bank-Industry Networks and Asymmetric Information between Creditors

Differences between financial systems are relevant to the analysis of real economic growth, because banks have an advantage as information producers concerning their client firms (Campbell and Kracaw, 1980, Diamond, 1984, and Fama, 1985). Banks have private information, while investors in corporate bonds only have public information (MacKie-Mason, 1989, and Sharpe, 1990). If banker-entrepreneur interaction is institutionalized in a bank-industry network, based on mutual trust and network commitment, then the banker may produce private information through learning-by-financing, the function of the bank-industry network.

My concept learning-by-financing represents Adam's and Farber's (1988) financial feedback loops of venture capital finance, which occur after each phase of the innovation process.[2] Hence, learning-by-financing is conceptually related to Arrow's (1962) learning-by-doing and Lundberg's (1961) Horndal effect, because the output of financial information increases for the same input of human capital in banking.[3] This reduces the banker's information costs and thereby the entrepreneur's financing costs.

The private information obtained through learning-by-financing is an outcome of a continuous interaction in a durable relationship between banker and entrepreneur. In the sense of Polanyi (1967), the private information is tacit, making a transformation into public information available at the financial markets impossible. Learning-by-financing should, therefore, be distinguished from credit-rating based on public information.

Learning-by-financing within bank-industry networks is a conceptual means to explain how resource allocation in a credit-based financial system differ from resource allocation in a capital market-based system. Berglöf (1990) explains system differences on the basis of their distributions of control rights, using a property rights approach, but does not consider asymmetric information. My explanation will, however, be based on asymmetric information in an evolutionary context. Learning-by-financing implies a capacity to keep information asymmetries low by adapting to change. Lock-in (David, 1985, Arthur, 1988) into previously successful choices, studied by Glete (1998) and Ballot and Taymaz (1998), is avoided, as long as learning-by-financing remains efficient. Networks create a critical mass of adopters rather than lock-in, along the lines of Witt (1997).

Japan can be regarded as the stronghold of the credit-based system or bank convention and the USA as the stronghold of the capital market-based system or bond convention. According to Porter (1992), the capital market is characterized by dedicated capital in Japan, where owners are permanent with corporate perpetuity as goal, and by fluid capital in the USA, where owners are transient in their search for high returns on investment and high current stock prices. The high bank-industry cross-holding of shares and the high reliance on bank loans in Japan reflect lower information asymmetries, thus reducing the "lemon's" costs when financing investments (Becchetti, 1995). Hence, learning-by-financing within bank-industry networks may explain the low information costs of the banker.

The stable relationships of credit-based systems provide a better framework for innovation strategies in which firm-specific assets are important (OECD, 1995). Learning-by-financing guides the resource allocation of firm-specific assets, often being tacit. Furthermore, bank-industry networks allow for network-specific assets. The Japanese keiretsu improves innovation appropriability through a broader technological base (OECD, 1995). Knowledge diffusion occurs through the network links, thus being reserved for network members.

The bank-industry network consists of links between the banker and a set of entrepreneurs and links between the entrepreneurs based on a sequence of complementarities. The sequence of complementarities form a development block where financiers coordinate entrepreneurial activities

(Dahmén, 1950, 1988). During Sweden's industrialization in the late 19th and early 20th century, banks financed entire development blocks, e.g. both users and producers of the engineering industry (Nygren, 1983).

Under uncertainty, the network is a device to internalize externalities for members (Teubal and Zuscovitch, 1994). In this context, uncertainty is genuine and differs from calculable risk, along the lines of Knight (1921). A privileged group maintains its stability by producing a joint product of private and public goods (Sandler, 1992). Bank-industry networks are privileged groups where the banker's learning-by-financing concerning each individual entrepreneur benefits from the learning across all links between the banker and the set of entrepreneurs belonging to the network.

Learning-by-financing is the function on which bank-industry networks are founded. Institutions provide heuristics reducing uncertainty (Hodgson, 1989). Institutions, such as the firm, the bank-industry network, the organized capital market and moral values, may transform uncertainty to subjective risk. Based on Knight's (1921) distinction between uncertainty and risk, Eliasson (1990) considers firms as competent teams whose function is to transform uncertainty to subjective risk, thus enabling entrepreneurs to deal with mistakes. However, the firm is just one kind of institution. As Granovetter (1995) points out, firms form cooperative relations within business groups linked by relations of interpersonal trust, i.e. what I call bank-industry networks. Firms may not be a sufficient response to uncertainty. Business failures give costs of organizational learning (Eliasson, 1992) and organizational competence requires a capacity to integrate production between firms (Eliasson, 1996). The bank-industry network can be seen as a set of interdependent competent teams in which firm competence depends on complementarities.

According to Rivaud-Danset and Salais (1992), an industrial finance convention with long-term bank-industry links and mutual understanding opens up for greater industrial flexibility under uncertainty. Banks may informationally capture high quality firms through a history of information production at low cost (Fama, 1985, and Sharpe, 1990). If risks are calculable, then this means a risk reduction for the banker. In the case of genuine uncertainty, however, the bank-industry network reduces uncertainty through the heuristics derived from learning-by-financing. According to Heiner (1988a), agents have a sufficient ability to filter through an evolutionary selection process including delayed adjustment of imperfect decisions, as long as reliability is greater than the minimum reliability for improvement. Referring to Heiner's (1988b) notion of imperfect use of imperfect information, the imperfect decision making reliability of the banker increases through learning-by-financing, thus increasing decision flexibility.

1.2.3 Network Commitment and Dynamic Transaction Costs in the Evolution of Bank-Industry Networks

Institutions, including moral values, influence economic behavior. Moral values establish the trust which is necessary for cooperation of interdependent agents within bank-industry networks. Cooperation may evolve without formal contracts (Witt, 1986). In fact, networks do not require formal contracts (Håkansson, 1989), but mutual trust and network commitment are crucial. Granovetter (1985) considers explicit and implicit contracts as substitutes for trust. Lundvall (1991) points out that historically involved mutual trust decreases transaction costs. The role of trust is to reduce conflicts (Granovetter, 1985) and uncertainty (Whitley, 1992). According to Granovetter (1985), economic behavior is embedded in social relations which generate trust. As shown by Coleman (1988), social capital which is embodied in social relations may contribute to the formation of human capital.

Taking Japan as an example, one may argue that Japanese society has provided network commitment as an institutional endowment of social capital which has contributed to learning-by-financing. The Japanese keiretsu is a business group of interdependent firms, not a hierarchical business group, such as the South Korean chaebol (Granovetter, 1995). Interdependence requires mutual trust and network commitment. According to Fukuyama (1995), Japan is a high-trust society which reduces transaction costs. Commitment and loyalty facilitate information sharing (Whitley, 1990). The Tokugawa Shogunate was characterized by collective loyalties, both within villages as well as at the national level where collective loyalty was a prerequisite for peace (Whitley, 1992). Hence, network commitment based on collective loyalty has been an institutional endowment of Japanese society.

My approach is through network commitment a synthesis between economic theory and what Mizruchi and Stearns (1994) refer to as the sociological view. Cultural embeddedness and social networks, in particular the stabilizing effects of a high density of interaction, are brought into an evolutionary economic model. In this evolutionary context, bankers and entrepreneurs are assumed to follow satisficing rules. According to Etzioni (1988), moral values decrease decision making costs. An explanation is provided by Frank (1988) who argues that moral sentiment induces commitment. Network commitment is a moral commitment rule which represents what Sugden (1991) calls a resolute behavior of pragmatic rationality. Network commitment provides the social capital which is necessary to create durable interpersonal links through social interaction.

Bank-industry networks evolve through a history of successful banker-entrepreneur interaction, establishing durable links between bankers and entrepreneurs who are the nodes of the network. Economic networks are formed by agents who invest in links between themselves, thereby creating sunk costs inducing stability of the links (Johansson and Westin, 1994, Karlsson and Westin, 1994). The networks, being based on interpersonal trust, constitute business groups which decrease transaction costs through inter-firm cooperative relations (Whitley, 1992).

Transaction costs are reduced by vertical integration, as contractual arrangement, thus solving a Prisoners' Dilemma problem (Bjuggren, 1985). Following Langlois and Robertson (1995), networks are business institutions which reduce dynamic transaction costs of economic change to the extent that they solve a Coordination problem under genuine uncertainty without market contracts which are too costly. In this context, dynamic transaction costs are created by the innovation process itself as costs of innovation.

The reduction of dynamic transaction costs is the function of the networks which evolve through social interaction. There are, nevertheless, dynamic transaction costs of banker-entrepreneur interaction. For the experimentally organized economy, Eliasson (1992) considers the costs of business failures as costs of organizational learning. In my analysis, however, the costs of business failure are a consequence of dynamic transaction costs of banker-entrepreneur interaction, but all bankers and entrepreneurs face them, irrespective of their cooperating within networks or their remaining independent. Lock-in into inefficient networks would be the only additional interaction cost of bank-industry networks. The emphasis of credit-based systems in innovation strategies based on firm-specific assets decreases the flexibility in technology choices (OECD, 1995). This imposes some inertia in the transition between technologies. For firms, Eliasson (1996) argues that new solutions through entry, reorganization, rationalization, and exit are necessary when successful choices of the past no longer work. The same holds for bank-industry networks, otherwise they would not remain an evolutionary viable convention.

Institutions are created as conventions, emerging from an evolutionary selection process (Schotter, 1981, Sugden, 1986). Given uncertainty and bounded rationality, I will analyze Schumpeterian banker-entrepreneur interaction as an evolutionary Stag Hunt game. According to this game, the banker and the entrepreneur would be better off by cooperating within a bank-industry network, but only if both of them do so. The Stag Hunt game is an intermediary game between the Prisoners' Dilemma game and the Coordination game (Ullmann-Margalit, 1977). Dynamic transaction costs are, thus, given appropriate attention.

Using Sugden's (1986) convention concept, the two evolutionary stable strategies of this game corresponds to the spontaneously evolved conventions of financing industrial innovations:

(i) The bank convention institutionalizes banker-entrepreneur interaction within bank-industry networks, establishing a durable link between bankers and entrepreneurs. Learning-by-financing is thereby made possible, so the banker may develop private information.

(ii) The bond convention institutionalizes banker-entrepreneur interaction as a market contract, establishing a temporary link. There is no learning-by-financing, so the banker has to rely on public information available at the market, performing a monitoring function.

The evolutionary viability of the bank convention is given by its relative fitness. The institutional dynamics of the banker and entrepreneur populations toward either the bank convention or the bond convention depend on the relative payoffs determined by learning-by-financing.

As bankers and entrepreneurs interact along each quality ladder of the economy, the institutional dynamics of the game of each quality ladder turn the financial system of the economy into a specific combination of the bank convention and the bond convention. The relative fitness of the bank convention is higher in a credit-based financial system, such as the Japanese one, compared to a market-based financial system, such as the American one.

1.3 Finance, Institutions, and Quality Ladders in Economic Growth: A Synthesis between Evolutionary Models and Endogenous Growth Models

Schumpeterian economic evolution has been analyzed by means of evolutionary economics where economic agents use satisficing rules,[4] and by means of the general equilibrium theory of endogenous growth with quality upgrading.[5]

My approach is evolutionary, since uncertainty and bounded rationality of the banker and the entrepreneur are recognized. Bankers and entrepreneurs are regarded as satisficing agents, along the lines of Simon (1959). Since I regard institutions as uncertainty reducing conventions providing satisficing rules, I share the approach of new institutional economics.[6] My explanation of the existence of bank-industry networks is functionalist-evolutionary.[7] Bank-industry networks evolve in my model, because they provide through learning-by-financing a higher relative fitness of bankers and entrepreneurs.

What determines the relative fitness of a convention, such as the bank convention characterized by learning-by-financing? The answer is the capacity to generate quality upgrading of the economic process, the foundation of economic evolution. Following Georgescu-Roegen (1971), the economy is regarded as an irrevocable process of transformation of free energy (resources) into bounded energy (waste), continuously increasing entropy, although to a smaller extent the higher the quality of the process. Quality upgrading implies that less free energy is used per utility unit produced by the economic process.

For a Georgescu-Roegen type of economy with qualitative growth, I extend the simple endogenous quality ladder model (Grossman and Helpman, 1991a) with systemic differences in learning-by-financing. Bankers may develop private information through learning-by-financing or act as investors in corporate bonds who only have public information. Asymmetric information between creditors having private information and creditors just having public information (MacKie-Mason, 1989, and Sharpe, 1990) is combined with investment determined by interest rate spreads (Gertler, Hubbard, and Kashyap, 1991).

Hence, my contribution is to add financial institutions to the Grossman-Helpman endogenous growth model with quality ladders, enlarging and enriching the model with institutional differences in

Schumpeterian banker-entrepreneur interaction and the consequences of bank-industry networks for growth regimes. An institutional explanation of innovativeness will thereby be given, since growth regimes are institutionally determined. The Grossman-Helpman model is helpful in identifying growth regimes, although it is neoclassical in its focus on equilibrium and optimization. As Witt (1996a) argues, evolutionary economics substitutes market process generating and disseminating novelty for equilibrium and transition laws for optimization. For clarity, the growth regimes are studied as equilibria, while the transition between growth regimes will be considered in the institutional analysis.

In an evolutionary setting, stressing the crucial role of institutions for growth regimes, there are two theoretical approaches which illustrate the importance of evolutionary viability of economic institutions.

Firstly, there is the neo-Schumpeterian long wave approach. The conjunction of the technological subsystem and the socio-institutional subsystem of the economy determines the ability of an economy to assimilate new technologies and, thereby, the path of economic evolution (Perez, 1983). The technological subsystem defines a paradigm, a cluster of technological trajectories which innovation follows as path-dependent process (Dosi, 1984).

Within the socio-institutional subsystem, a financial style (Santarelli 1989) is defined, since the emergence of a technological paradigm requires a new pattern of investments, something which becomes possible only after a qualitative change of the financial system. Thus, the conjunction of the two subsystems defines what Vercelli (1989) calls a technological-institutional paradigm which breaks down if the two subsystems are not sufficiently compatible.

Secondly, the French *régulation* approach tries to provide a system framework for economic evolution with interdependence between institutions, accumulation regimes, and economic change (Boyer, 1986). According to this approach, institutional forms determine a mode of régulation, reproducing basic relationships and maintaining the accumulation regime which defines the pattern of productive organization within firms. The mode of régulation and the accumulation regime determine together the mode of economic evolution. The economy shows structural fitness as long as these institutional forms are able to keep the functioning of *régulation* consistent with the institutional forms themselves and the accumulation regime.

Essentially, the two approaches tell the same story. The accumulation regime corresponds to the technological paradigm, while both the institutional forms and the modes of *régulation* correspond to the socio-institutional subsystem. The technological paradigm and the accumulation regime both refer to the growth regime, while the socio-institutional subsystem and the institutional forms with their modes of *régulation* both refer to the institutions.

The problem with both approaches is the lack of explanation of how institutions influence the growth regime. Institutions matter, but no theoretical explanation of how they matter is given.

Interaction would be a key to such an explanation. Interactive learning, institutionalized as bilateral governance structures, reduces transaction costs (Lundvall, 1991), thus extending the technological paradigm to a techno-economic paradigm which includes interfaces between users and producers (Andersen, 1991).

In my analysis, the growth regime consists of interfaces between bankers and entrepreneurs, yielding learning-by-financing when the interaction is durable with strong interfaces. What everything boils down to is the ability of banks to produce heuristics for innovation through the information production about entrepreneurial qualities of industrial firms as a continuous learning-by-financing process. They have to continuously develop their interfaces with the innovative industrial firms, thus making entrepreneurs go beyond what has been revealed by experience to support the development of unexplored opportunities. The successful choices of the past may result in failure if repeated (Eliasson, 1996). Hence, learning-by-financing has to adapt to economic evolution.

A continuous development of interfaces reflects a commitment to what Dosi (1990) calls the optimistic irrationality of the Schumpeterian entrepreneur, but might as well be considered as a resolute behavior of pragmatic rationality (Sugden, 1991). Such a commitment is essential to the evolutionary viability of bank-industry networks, thus illustrating the rationality of moral commitment. In other words, rational behavior may have a cultural foundation in the value systems.

Aoki (1988) compares the rational and cultural approaches to explain the Japanese economy, pointing at the rationality of Japanese institutions which combine decentralized information-processing with centralized incentive structures. In my analysis, however, the rationality of bank-industry networks and network commitment as institutions is at issue. Moral commitment in a bank-industry network is rational, because dynamic transaction costs become lower, increasing the value of information. Network commitment represents an institutional endowment whose rationality is seen in the evolution of the bank-industry networks.

My contribution is to analyze the evolution of bank-industry networks as an evolutionary Stag Hunt game to show the crucial role of institutional endowments, such as network commitment, to the process of institutional change. When network commitment has evolved for historical reasons, the institutional endowments are sufficient for the evolution of the bank convention by spontaneous order.

The evolution of bank-industry networks may follow two different conjectures - the two conjectures for analysis of the propagation process of economic institutions identified by Witt (1989) - depending on institutional endowments; the Smith-Menger-Hayek conjecture of spontaneous order, on the one hand, and the Olson-Buchanan-Tullock conjecture of collective action, on the other hand. In my analysis, these two conjectures are combined. I will argue that bank-industry networks evolved historically through spontaneous order in Sweden, while collective action was necessary in France.

The evolution of the securitized economy during the 1980s has imposed a challenge to the bank convention. Securitization involves the creation of an underlying portfolio with various classes of claims that are sold on the market. Minsky (1990) considers the greater variety of forms of financing as a positive consequence, while the strong emphasis on short-term profitability to sustain the claims may have a negative impact on the financing of long-term technological innovation.

Securitization with its underlying preference for exit rather than voice gives a short-term orientation which penalizes entrepreneurs, unless institutional investors restore the voice mechanism (Gönenç, 1988). Industrial investment becomes through securitization dependent on the collective opinion of financial market actors (OECD, 1995). The mode of investment decisions tend to become more capital market-oriented, thus reflecting the American way. The fluid capital of the USA, focusing on short-term appreciation of shares explains the short-term nature of investment horizons and R&D portfolios of American firms (Porter, 1992).

Hence, market pressures may render financial and industrial entrepreneurship incompatible by imposing too high short-term profitability requirements. Financial innovation decreases the maximum distance between different points in the yield-liquidity space of financial instruments, thus pushing up the yields required by the market (Desai and Low, 1987). Nevertheless, there are local bank-industry networks in the USA. Silicon Valley consists of innovative networks around venture capitalists (Langlois and Robertson, 1995). The US system seems better in funding emerging fields than in securing competitive positions through the upgrading of capabilities (Porter, 1992).

Financial innovation may increase the static efficiency of the industrial finance system, but decrease its dynamic efficiency. Static efficiency refers to optimization on existing knowledge, while dynamic efficiency refers to adaptation to assimilate new knowledge (Klein, 1977). Goldberg (1994) argues that a Faustian bargain has been made to reduce short-term transaction costs, but with increased financial fragility as the price of the bargain, thus making a case for autonomous local systems. A bank with private information may offer procedures to deal with volatile solvency, unknown to securities markets (Gönenç, 1991).

Bank-industry networks, as institutions reducing dynamic transaction costs of economic change, constitute autonomous local systems which make entrepreneurs less vulnerable to market pressures. My contribution is to analyze the viability of bank-industry networks organized around universal banks in a securitized economy with higher profitability requirements, focusing on network commitment as institutional endowment.

The theory will be illustrated by an empirical assessment of the differences between financial systems. The importance of collective action as propagation process for securitization will be assessed by comparing the viability of the bank convention in Sweden and France. As reference points, I will use the industrial finance systems of Japan with its strong bank convention and the USA with its strong bond convention.

Summing up, my contribution consists of three parts:

(i) Financial institutions are added to the Grossman-Helpman endogenous growth model with quality ladders, enlarging and enriching the model with institutional differences in Schumpeterian banker-entrepreneur interaction and the consequences of bank-industry networks for growth regimes.

(ii) The evolution of bank-industry networks is analyzed as an evolutionary Stag Hunt game to show the crucial role of institutional endowments, such as network commitment, to the process of institutional change which moves the economy between growth regimes. The model explains the propagation mechanisms behind the evolution of bank-industry networks. The

institutional endowments determine the extent to which propagation is guided by spontaneous order or collective action.
(iii) The viability of bank-industry networks organized around universal banks in a securitized economy with higher profitability requirements is analyzed theoretically through appreciative theorizing. Differences between financial systems are illustrated by an empirical assessment.

1.4 Structure of the Book

Chapter 2 develops the general argument for the view that the bank-industry network around a universal bank is viable as institutional form for industrial banking in a securitized economy. Bank-industry networks are analyzed with reference to their capacity to achieve a reconciliation between the short-term perspective of the financier in the securitized economy and the long-term perspective of the entrepreneur who needs intangible assets. In a securitized economy, such a reconciliation would increase the value of learning-by-financing.

Chapter 3 formalizes the systemic differences in learning-by-financing by extending the Grossman-Helpman model with asymmetric information. Growth regimes are compared by three numerical simulation rounds, starting with four variables and sixteen regimes. In order to see how the two financial variables determine quality increments and entry costs, the former is endogenized, giving eight regimes and three variables, and then the latter, giving four regimes and two variables.

Chapter 4 develops an evolutionary game-theoretic analysis of the evolution of bank-industry networks as a Stag Hunt game. The analysis demonstrates that the evolution is path-dependent and that the propagation mechanism is spontaneous order when the institutional endowments are sufficient and collective action when this is not the case. The theoretical model is then applied to explain the historical evolution of bank-industry networks in Sweden and France, comparing spontaneous order and collective action as propagation processes of institutional change.

Chapter 5 assesses the evolutionary viability of the bank convention in a securitized economy which evolved during the 1980s. A theoretical analysis is illustrated by an empirical assessment of the differences between financial systems, using macroeconomic financial indicators as well as capital structure and financing of non-financial corporations.

Chapter 6 gives a general conclusion concerning the evolutionary viability of bank-industry networks.

Notes

1. Output is seen as consumer utility produced.

2. Financial feedback is given after each financing phase; seed, start-up, expansion, and bridge. Continuous participation gives the banker the opportunity to gradually get to know the entrepreneur.

3. Lundberg observed pure productivity increases, i.e. productivity increases without net investments, for the Swedish iron work Horndal, where the same input of capital generated an increasing output. In this context, organizational routines matter. Learning-by-doing refers to the development of skills and their organization.

4. See Nelson and Winter (1982) and Iwai (1984a,b).

5. See Segerstrom, Anant, and Dinopoulos (1990) for a Schumpeterian product life cycle model and Aghion and Howitt (1992) for a Schumpeterian creative destruction model. Grossman and Helpman (1991a,b) have combined these two models into a single quality ladder model.

6. See e.g. Ullmann-Margalit (1977), Schotter (1981), Axelrod (1984), and Sugden (1986) who all use game theory to explain the evolution of institutions or rules.

7. See e.g. Langlois (1986) for a comparison between functional explanations focusing on why institutions exist and causal-genetic explanations focusing on how they have emerged. Although both are valuable, the former opens up for a comparison between spontaneous order and collective action through the connection between function and intention.

2 Credit, Innovation, and the Evolutionary Viability of Universal Banks in a Securitized Economy

2.1 Universal Banking, Bank-Industry Networks, and the Securitized Economy

There are close links between financial innovation and capital formation (Viñals and Berges, 1988). As a consequence of financial innovation during the last two decades, the securitized economy evolved during the 1980s. Securitization means that lending to investments is financed through the creation of an underlying portfolio for a set of financial instruments that are sold on the market with various classes of claims to the cash flow of the portfolio. Industrial investment becomes through securitization dependent on the collective opinion of financial market actors (OECD, 1995).

According to Minsky (1990), a greater variety of forms of financing is a positive consequence of securitization, while the strong emphasis on short-term profitability to sustain the claims may have a negative impact on the financing of long-term technological innovation. Securitization with its underlying preference for exit rather than voice gives a short-term orientation which penalizes entrepreneurs, unless institutional investors restore the voice mechanism (Gönenç, 1988).

Porter (1992) explains the short-term nature of investment horizons and R&D portfolios of American firms by the fluid capital, focusing on short-term appreciation of shares, of the USA. Institutional investors, such as pension funds, who prefer the exit mechanism have a short-term orientation to their investments in long-term securities, thus increasing the short-term profitability an industrial investment with long-term securities as sources of finance is required to show. In financial systems with dedicated capital, however, the institutional investors have a preference for the voice mechanism and a long-term orientation to industrial investments.

According to OECD (1989c), the short-term perspective of the financier may be reconciled with the long-term perspective of the entrepreneur through active owners and informed creditors. Financial institutions and large enterprises may develop into institutional investors, in order to assume the role of active owners. Banks may assume the role of informed creditors in order to sell know-how to their large client enterprises and concentrate their financing of industry to small and medium-sized enterprises, since securitization would be too expensive for the latter.

The growing importance of intangible investments to develop firm-specific know-how may be facilitated through the financing by securities, because risk-spreading becomes easier (OECD, 1987b, 1989c, Gönenç, 1988), but the globalization of financial markets penalizes intangible investments (OECD, 1995). Securitization tends to strengthen the exit mechanism (Gönenç, 1988). Yet, bank financing of intangible investments may strengthen bank-industry links (Pastré, 1986). Private information developed by a bank concerning an industrial client offers procedures to deal with volatile solvency, unknown to securities markets (Gönenç, 1991). Learning-by-financing is a prerequisite for the voice mechanism and provides a risk-reducing mechanism, thus supporting intangible investments.

The universal bank combines commercial and investment banking within one banking firm and may have direct or indirect control over equity in industrial firms. The German system is characterized by bank-industry networks around universal banks, while the main banks of the Japanese bank-industry networks, called keiretsu, are specialized banks. The Japanese keiretsu is, however, characterized by very strong links between banks, securities houses, and industrial enterprises (Gerlach, 1992). With respect to bank-industry links, universality can, therefore, be achieved within the keiretsu as a bank-industry network.

The purpose of this chapter is to develop the general argument for the view that the bank-industry network around a universal bank is viable as an institutional form for industrial banking in a securitized economy.

The following two aspects will be discussed:

(i) The ability of universal banks to adapt to the securitized economy so as to exploit the new economic opportunities and increase the capacity of the banking system to finance industrial innovation.

(ii) The comparative advantage of universal banks in reconciling financial and industrial entrepreneurship.

Section 2.2 deals with the dynamic efficiency of universal banking.

Section 2.3 introduces the differences in learning-by-financing between various financial systems. Section 2.4 studies the evolution of the securitized economy, while section 2.5 considers qualitative change in banking. Section 2.6 gives a summary.

2.2 The Dynamic Efficiency of Universal Banking

The dynamic efficiency of universal banking was apparent in Schumpeter's (1911) theory of economic evolution. The theory has its historical foundations. The crucial role Schumpeter (1911) gave credit creation and banker in the innovation process, is based upon the economic history of Schumpeter's own time. The industrial expansion of Germany with very close bank-industry links institutionalized in the German universal bank, could be compared to the failure of the Austro-Hungarian bankers to establish industrial banking in the anti-entrepreneurial Austria-Hungary.[1]

In Germany, the bankers had, what Sejersted (1988) in a historical comparison between Norwegian and Swedish banking refers to as legitimacy to be coordinators (industrial strategists) at the mesoeconomic level. In Austria-Hungary, this was not the case.

Sejersted's comparison is interesting here, as the Swedish and German industrial banking systems as well as industrial structures are very similar. Sweden produced a successful industrial banking system, like Germany, something which was not the case in Norway, where Swedish industrial banks exploited the business opportunities to establish themselves.

The reason behind the difference in the evolution of industrial banking was, according to Sejersted (1988), that the Norwegian central bank was too dominant during the 19th century, while the Swedish central bank did leave open space for private banks to emerge. Attempts to establish some kind of French *banque d'affaire* in Norway did not work very well, nor did the attempts to copy the Swedish model.

Hence, the main difference was whether the state had allowed the banks to perform a function, historically proving their capacity to coordinate. The evolution of German universal banking was, naturally, connected with the unification of Germany and the parallel financial and political unification (Kindleberger, 1984). Therefore, the relative strength in the historical relations between banking and government is of great importance. In the history of qualitative changes in the financial systems from Schumpeter's time to ours, new institutional forms for financing innovation have arisen, together with new needs. The issue is whether universal banks are evolutionary viable, maintaining a sufficient dynamic efficiency, for financing innovation in the securitized economy.

Allocative efficiency which refers to the capacity to allocate scarce savings into the investments yielding the highest social returns, and technical or cost efficiency which refers to the capacity in doing this to minimum cost (OECD 1987b, 1989b). Allocative efficiency may be dynamic as well as static. Following Klein's (1977) definition of dynamic efficiency, an industrial finance system has to allocate the economy's financial resources to industrial innovation in such a way that industry may efficiently absorb new knowledge, i.e. enhance its capacity to adapt to the changing economic opportunity set. Dosi (1990) argues that this process requires allocation-by-exploration as well as allocation-by-selection.

Financial entrepreneurship, leading to new financial instruments, may increase the technical efficiency and static allocative efficiency, referring to allocation-by-selection. Industrial entrepreneurship requires dynamic allocative efficiency where allocation-by-exploration is combined with allocation-by-selection. Innovative success requires the financial system to allow for some industrial experimentation and failure without making itself fragile. Learning-by-financing refers to a process which is able to combine financial stability and industrial experimentation.

2.3 Differences in Learning-by-Financing between Financial Systems

In the literature, financial systems are considered to be either capital market-based or credit-based. Gurley and Shaw (1955) show that economic evolution is retarded without financial intermediation and that commercial banks create credit to the extent that is determined by the relative preference for deposits and currency compared to other financial assets. Hence, if there is a high preference for money compared to securities which are close substitutes for money, the system would be more credit-based.

According to Gurley and Shaw (1955), financial intermediation, i.e. indirect external finance, is a prerequisite for growth, because otherwise money supply is kept constant, thus increasing interest rates and retarding economic growth. Hence, credit is necessary. Financial instruments which are close substitutes for money would, however, decrease the need for a higher money supply. In this case, the system would be more capital market-based. Financial intermediaries would be relatively more involved in securities business.

Financial intermediation differs not so much in extent between systems, but in institutional form. Market-based systems favor the exit mechanism and have specialized, risk-spreading intermediaries, while credit-based systems favor the voice mechanism and are characterized by universal banks and mesoeconomic ownership and control systems sharing risks (Berglöf, 1988).[2] From the perspective of corporate control, the bank-industry network could be regarded as such a mesoeconomic ownership and control system, but my analysis emphasizes coordination through interaction under genuine uncertainty.

2.3.1 A Taxonomy of Financial Systems

Zysman (1983) identifies three different types of financial systems:
(i) The capital market-based system, whose adjustment strategy is company-led, allocates by the price mechanism of competitive markets. Long-term industrial funding is provided by securities at the stock and bond markets, while bank lending is short-term. There are weak links between the central bank and the commercial banks, the former being a limited lender of last resort.
(ii) The credit-based system with government-administered prices, whose adjustment strategy is state-led, allocates by prices set by government. Credit is the core of industrial funding. The government supports money creation to increase industrial credit and sets prices to influence the allocation process. There are strong links between the central bank and the commercial banks, as refinancing with the central bank is essential.
(iii) The negotiated credit-based system allocates by negotiation. Credit is the core and the system resembles the credit-based system with government-administered prices, but with the important difference that the allocation process is determined by negotiations between the dominant institutions at the market.

Bank-industry networks, in their capacity of being the dominant institutions of a negotiated credit-based system, have a stronger coordinating function in conjunction with the tripartite (corporatist) policy-making arrangements. The government cannot directly influence the allocation, but has to form coalitions with interest organizations and bank-industry networks, e.g. in Germany and Sweden.

Over time, these three types of financial systems change and converge into hybrid, or mixed, forms. This should be seen as a necessary adaptation, since an important aspect of the evolutionary viability of financial institutions is their capacity of adapting and transforming the financial system to better meet the needs of the continuously evolving economy.

2.3.2 Learning-by-Financing Efficiency and the System-Specific Natural Rate of Indebtedness

The difference in financial intermediation between financial systems is qualitative rather than quantitative, being reflected in different learning-by-financing potential for institutional reasons. Learning-by-financing is a kind of interactive learning. Lundvall (1991) argues that interactive learning is institutionalized as bilateral governance structures. According to OECD (1995), the stable bilateral relations in credit-based financial systems create discipline, favoring innovation strategies based on firm-specific assets.

Bank-industry networks make the interaction between banker and entrepreneur durable with strong interfaces, so that the banker over time develops private information. The continuous interaction allows for better resource allocation through investments in firm-specific assets. Hence, the banker performs a venture capital function and the entrepreneur may pursue the unexplored opportunities created by the firm-specific assets.

According to Zysman (1983), credit-based systems use a venture capital approach, stressing future prospects and projected cash flow, while capital market-based systems resort to the pawnbroker approach, where historic performance and collateral are important. Porter's (1992) distinction between dedicated and fluid capital provides an explanation. Dedicated capital implies stable owners, while fluid capital implies transient owners. Stable ownership links contribute to the strong bank-industry links in credit-based systems (OECD, 1995). Hence, stable debt and equity allow banks to perform a venture capital function. Arguing along the lines of Dosi (1990), the venture capital approach is an outcome of the integration of allocation-by-selection and allocation-by-exploration within German universal banks, while these allocation mechanisms are separated in the USA with its separate venture capital industry.

Indirect finance implies credit rationing (Gurley and Shaw, 1955).

According to Stiglitz and Weiss (1981), banks try to avoid adverse selection, since a higher interest rate may increase the failure rate and decrease bank profits. Their model gives underinvestment result with equity as preferred method of finance, because the marginal project financed has the highest success probability. The Stiglitz-Weiss model can be compared to the model developed by de Meza and Webb (1987) which yields overinvestment results with debt as preferred method of finance, because the marginal project has the lowest success probability. Hence, in a credit-based system with universal banks, there is continuous overinvestment which should be seen as an investment in the future, an allocation to explore new possibilities. This is what Dosi (1990) means by the banks' integrating selection and exploration when allocating funds.

The integration of allocation-by-selection and allocation-by-exploration yield learning-by-financing, something which explains why a high debt/equity ratio is consistent with financial stability. A banker with close links to industry may, as insider, hold an "insider's stake" of wealth at risk in the firm. According to Bernanke and Gertler (1990), financial stability increases when the banker has an "insider's stake" in the entrepreneurial effort, while the use of arm's length financing made possible by securitization turns the bankers into outsiders, something which increases financial fragility. Hence, the "insider's stake" is an outcome of learning-by-financing within bank-industry networks.

Financial stability contributes positively to industrial innovation, because a more long-term perspective become possible. Learning-by-financing of universal banks increases financial stability, thus creating a higher potential for compatibility between financial and industrial entrepreneurship. Securitization would decrease this compatibility through increased financial fragility which induces short-term thinking.

Minsky (1990) argues for state intervention to support industrial entrepreneurship in the securitized economy. This kind of intervention would, of course, be unnecessary as long as the universal banks perform their function as industrial coordinators, instead of becoming short-term speculators. As Gönenç (1988) points out, institutional investors may contribute in a similar fashion through the voice mechanism. The key is the "insider's stake" created through leaning-by-financing

Differences in learning-by-financing between financial systems give system-specific natural rates of indebtedness, being the long-run, maximum sustainable debt/equity ratio in a financial system. A high debt/equity ratio reflects efficient learning-by-financing which allows bankers to keep their information costs and entrepreneurs' financing costs low.

McCauley and Zimmer (1989) find that Japan had lower cost of capital for industrial R&D projects with 10 year payoff lag during the 1977-1989 period, because the keiretsu reduces risk, thus making a higher debt/equity ratio compatible with financial stability. Consequently, a lower cost of equity is observed for Japanese banks than US banks during the 1984-1990 period (Zimmer and McCauley, 1991). According to OECD (1995), there has been some convergence of overall cost of capital, but differences between financial systems remain, since attentive and well-informed financial institutions may handle the uncertainty in R&D financing and the cash requirement peaks of the innovation process in a better way.

2.4 The Evolution of the Securitized Economy

The evolution of the securitized economy is the history of qualitative change in the financial system, an incomplete transformation of industrial finance regimes. In capital market-based systems, Minsky (1990) sees a transformation from Managerial Capitalism to Managed Money Capitalism, which reduces the independence of corporate management. This corresponds to the change in financial style noted by Santarelli (1989). In credit-based financial systems, however, the bank-industry networks have been challenged by the securitized economy (Berglöf, 1988, Engwall and Johanson, 1989).

2.4.1 Finance and the Growing Need for Flexibility when Structural Uncertainty Increases

The evolution of the securitized economy coincided with financial deregulation which opened up the securities markets. The financial deregulation process can be linked to the increased structural uncertainty caused by the crisis which developed in the 1970s. As Europe gradually caught up with the USA, productivity slowed down and wage inflation followed (OECD, 1987b). The era of high growth and low inflation of the 1960s, turned into one of low growth, high inflation and high unemployment of the 1970s. Greater industrial flexibility was needed to meet technological uncertainties, but this created a demand for a more flexible financial system (Santarelli, 1989, Vercelli, 1989, OECD, 1989b).

In addition, the higher and more volatile inflation rates led to a strong liquidity preference increasing debt through a strong expansion of banks' balance sheet operations without a corresponding expansion in the capital base (OECD 1985). Various hedging instruments developed, following the deregulation of interest rates (OECD 1987b, 1989b). High and volatile rates of inflation, interest, and exchange rates created a demand for flexible instruments.

Competition in financial intermediation due to the emergence of non-banking financial institutions increased and intermediation patterns changed, thus improving financial flexibility. This gave the large firms an advantage, as Vercelli points out, because they had a stronger position vis-à-vis financial institutions.

Government deregulation and competition policies in the financial markets have, been important sources behind the change in the financial markets (OECD 1987b). Deregulation involved (i) deregulation of interest rates, (ii) deregulation of financial service prices, (iii) decompartmentalization of markets (more important where specialization used to be strong), and (iv) opening up to foreign competition.

Financial innovation since the 1970s has produced many new instruments and new markets. The new instruments are negotiable at secondary markets and liquid, thus reducing financial risks. Marketable securities provide for industrial risk spreading and flexible risk management (OECD, 1985, 1987b, Gönenç, 1988, Aglietta, Brender, and Coudert, 1990, Minsky, 1990). Securitization does, however, not necessarily imply the end of banking in favor of direct finance, as the banks themselves may learn how to use the new instruments to their own advantage.

2.4.2 Institutional Change within Financial Systems: Specialization and Diversification

The evolution of the securitized economy led to the emergence of non-bank financial institutions keeping their portfolio on the market. Great concern has been raised about their excessive reliance on short-term financial indicators by Gönenç (1988) and Minsky (1990). Financial and industrial entrepreneurship are not sufficiently compatible, according to Minsky (1990).

My argument is that this compatibility depends on the institutional forms for their interaction, because bank-industry networks and universal banking create financial stability and thereby investment in firm-specific assets. The private information developed by a bank with close links to its industrial clients offers procedures of monitoring and assistance, unknown to securities markets (Gönenç, 1991).

Without a tradition of involvement in industrial development, non-bank financial institutions would not have much of an incentive to regard investment in industrial innovation different than one in financial instruments. In addition, securitization allows large industrial firms to use direct finance (OECD 1989c), something which is a challenge to bank-industry networks.

Securitization provides a greater financial opportunity set for financial institutions with innovative commitment. Securities underwriting, a task for investment banks, is effective as means for governments and firms to obtain long-term debt or equity on a permanent basis (OECD 1986). Hence, for universal banks there are opportunities to preserve bank-industry networks through their investment bank function, still preserving the deposit base in the commercial bank function.

On the real side, there has been a revival of innovative entrepreneurship in a decentralized form which characterizes new high-tech firms (Vercelli 1989). However, this process does not mean that an innovative industrial structure has to be characterized by many small firms, because large firms have decentralized economic decision making about innovation and production within their internal organization.

In order to maintain a high level of industrial flexibility, intangible investments to create firm-specific know-how have become a major aspect of corporate strategy (OECD, 1987b, 1989c, Gönenç, 1988). Internal financing is desirable for firm-specific assets, such as the intangible ones. If external financing is necessary, then financing by securities would be suitable in order to spread risk. Banks have, therefore, an opportunity to finance intangible, firm-specific assets through loan syndication and securitization. As Pastré (1986) argues, bank financing of intangible investments is an outstanding means to strengthen bank-industry links.

Bank-industry networks allow for network-specific intangible assets, since there are opportunities for specialization and division of competence within a bank-industry network. Innovation appropriability may improve through a broader technological base (OECD, 1995). Knowledge diffusion occurs along the network links between the members of the network. Thus, a universal bank, as network bank, would then have a comparative advantage in financing innovation,[3] because the bank-industry networks give the necessary stability for investment in intangible investments. Porter (1992) explains the favorable investment climate for intangible investment in Japan and Germany by the dedicated capital and the corporate perpetuity objective of these two countries.

In addition, the greater the universality of banking, the more freedom the banks have to exploit the opportunities given by securitization. In this respect, one can agree with Pastré (1986), who argues that the involvement of banks with securities trading and off-balance sheet assets has made the distinction between market-based and credit-based economies artificial. Nevertheless, the difference between national financial systems still remain, being reflected in the national technological specialization (OECD, 1995).

During the 1980s, universality in banking increased through diversification. The trend to intra-sectoral diversification in the financial markets was very strong (Pastré, 1986, Gönenç, 1988, Muldur, 1990). In their search for external growth opportunities, banks were also involved in inter-sectoral diversification between banking, securities, and insurance (Muldur 1990). Thus, securitization does not seem to involve a crowding out of banks, but rather diversification even beyond the universal bank.

Yet, diversification has its limitations. Diversification has been used by well-established universal banks, while newcomers on the markets, including universal banks going abroad, have tended to specialize (OECD, 1992). Bank-industry networks with learning-by-financing seems to be a prerequisite for a diversification strategy, while entrants have to specialize.

2.5 Qualitative Change in Banking and the Securitized Economy

2.5.1 The Comparative Advantage of Universal Banks

In a securitized economy, banks have a considerable comparative advantage in financing innovation. Their deposit base make them able to take liquidity risks, thus supporting innovation and economic growth. According to Aglietta, Brender, and Coudert (1990), the aim of the banker's profession is to yield entrepreneurial rents, because banks are able to create credit. Banks lend money which eventually will come back as deposits, thus allowing them to assume the liquidity risk. In this way, banks differ from other financial institutions. Universal banks would, therefore, be viable, but the possibilities of risk-spreading through securitization has led to arguments in favor of a securitized system with specialized banks.

Steinherr and Huveneers (1990) argue for the superiority of a securitized system with a lending bank without a deposit base and total separation between commercial and investment banking to reduce risk, giving lower capital requirements and better maturity matching than today. What would happen with allocation-by-exploration in such a system? Would such a bank take liquidity risk without having a deposit base? If so, the risk would be even greater in a securitized system.

Their case is based on the assumption that the exit mechanism's being superior to the voice mechanism. From a principal-agent perspective, they argue that universal banks throw good money after bad. From an evolutionary perspective, however, this phenomenon indicates that universal banks have a sufficiently strong innovative commitment to make financial and industrial entrepreneurship compatible by allocating funds to exploration.

Steinherr and Huveneers (1990), in spite of their being critical towards universal banking, admit that universal banks have played a major role in maintaining the profit orientation of large corporations in Germany. According to them, universal banking seems to become the European convention of industrial banking. However, they turn that into a regulatory problem of free cash flows, because the positive contribution of universal banking may reflect higher debt/equity ratios or non-competitive rents. Free cash flow might be a problem in a static principal-agent world. From an evolutionary perspective, however, these non-competitive rents to which a high debt/equity ratio contributes, can be seen as the entrepreneurial rent necessary for dynamic efficiency.

The free cash flow makes experimentation possible, while maintaining a stable financial system. Bankers who are insiders in industry through learning-by-financing may allow free cash flow for the exploration of new opportunities. As insiders, they may assume higher liquidity risks. Banks with an "insider's stake" of wealth at risk in the firms contribute to financial stability (Bernanke and Gertler, 1990). The German universal bank has such an "insider stake" through its participation in industry with votes and proxy-votes.

The free cash flow is created through the kind of capital market disequilibrium discussed by Wicksell (1898, 1906). The Wicksellian capital market disequilibrium is a prerequisite for entrepreneurial profits and thereby innovation (Eliasson 1985). Innovation increases the natural rate of interest relative to the market rate of interest, something which in the longer run, induces credit rationing,[4] unless the banker receives an "insider's stake" in the entrepreneurial profit. A universal bank with close links to industry would, therefore, have an advantage compared to specialized banks, as illustrated by French banking.

The specialization, imposed by the government in France, contributed to a very high dependence of banking profits on interest rates, thus creating a strong incentive to diversify, as diversification may decrease this dependence (Pastré 1986). French banks have gradually turned into institutional investors (Pastré, 1992).

Yet, specialization may sometimes be advantageous, as shown by the performance of specialized, local bank-industry networks in the USA. Silicon Valley consists of innovative networks around venture capitalists (Langlois and Robertson, 1995). The US system seems better in funding emerging fields than in securing competitive positions through the upgrading of capabilities (Porter, 1992). Referring to Witt (1997), one may say that bank-industry networks around venture capitalists have a lower critical mass of adopters of emerging technologies than bank-industry networks around universal banks which focus on the upgrading of capabilities inherent in intangible, firm- and network-specific assets.

2.5.2 Banks and Corporate Finance in a Securitized Economy

During the 1980s, banks became involved with a very wide range of financial instruments and off-balance sheet activities. The development of asset and liability management increased the role of securities, making deposits less important for funding (OECD, 1985, 1987a). Securitization blurred the distinction between commercial banking and investment banking, as the range of activities increased (OECD, 1987a), suggesting a movement towards universal banking. The increased competition in banking through securitization forced banks to improve the technical efficiency of financial intermediation. An adaptation to the securitized economy became necessary to maintain vital bank-industry networks (Engwall and Johanson, 1989).

Adaptation has occurred. The shorter investment renewal cycles in industry increased bank involvement in corporate affairs with an expansion in bank medium-term lending to industry and a growing demand for investment banking services (OECD, 1989a). These services include financial and organizational restructuring, mergers and acquisitions, management buy-outs, and general advisory services to industrial firms. According to OECD (1995), attentive and well-informed financial institutions would be more able to meet the cash requirement peaks due to the increased R&D costs and the shortening of the product cycle. Hence, the bank-industry network around a universal bank has shown an ability to adapt and to maintain lower dynamic transaction cost through learning-by-financing within a bank-industry network.

2.6 Summary

The issue of this chapter has been the institutional reconciliation between the short-term perspective of the financier in the securitized economy and the long-term perspective of the entrepreneur to whom intangible investments are important.

Reasons have been given why the bank-industry network around a universal bank is viable as an institutional form for industrial banking in a securitized economy. Universal banks are able to adapt to the securitized economy and have a comparative advantage in reconciling financial and industrial entrepreneurship.

The general argument is that learning-by-financing within a bank-industry network allow for financial stability as well as industrial experimentation. This explains why universal banking integrates allocation-by-exploration with allocation-by-selection by relying on the voice mechanism rather than the exit mechanism of securities markets. Industrial enterprises may benefit from a higher debt/equity ratio without decreasing financial stability.

The evolution of the securitized economy has meant a diversification in banking. Universal banking seems to have been able to support the growing need for industrial flexibility within a mixed credit- and market-based financial system. The key factor is that the learning-by-financing within bank-industry networks decrease market pressures and make debt a more accessible source of finance to industry.

Notes

1. See Schumpeter (1939), Tilly (1986), Talele (1988), and Santarelli (1989) for the German bank as a model, and Streissler (1982) for the argument that Schumpeter's theory was an anti-theory to the anti-entrepreneurial, aristocratic Austria-Hungary. The banker, as the only really respectable businessman, had to take responsibility for economic evolution.

2. The distinction between the exit and voice mechanisms is originally due to Hirschman (1970) and is frequently referred to in the literature comparing market-based and credit-based financial systems. By focusing upon the functioning and evolution of bank-industry networks with universal banks, I analyze the voice mechanism as an institutional form.

3. Minsky (1990) characterizes the Schumpeterian banker as investment banker and the Keynesian one as commercial banker. Minsky's underlying argument for integrating the Schumpeterian vision into a Keynesian framework, suggest that universal banking would be appropriate.

4. This type of credit rationing should not be confused with the notion of credit rationing developed by Stiglitz and Weiss (1981), where fear of adverse selection at higher interest rates is the major source.

3 An Endogenous Growth Model with Asymmetric Information and Systemic Differences in Learning-by-Financing

3.1 Entropy, Quality Upgrading, and Finance

Endogenous growth models, such as the model developed by Grossman and Helpman (1991a), are general equilibrium patent race models with perfect foresight. My purpose is, however, to introduce asymmetric information as well as money and finance. The Grossman-Helpman quality ladder model[1] (Grossman and Helpman, 1991a) is extended with asymmetric information between creditors in order to analyze the implications of systemic differences in learning-by-financing for various growth regimes. By doing this, I am able to explain the function of bank-industry networks in industrial innovation in terms of private information.

I will use the extended Grossman-Helpman model to identify growth regimes, although it is neoclassical in its focus on equilibrium and optimization. As Witt (1996a) argues, evolutionary economics substitutes market process generating and disseminating novelty for equilibrium and transition laws for optimization. Nevertheless, growth regimes can be studied as equilibria, while institutional change gives transition between growth regimes. In chapter 4, I will formalize institutional change in an evolutionary game-theoretic setting.

Endogenous growth models with quality upgrading focus on vertical product differentiation which increases the relative efficiency of the economic process, thus saving free energy and thereby reducing the increase of entropy, in the sense of Georgescu-Roegen (1971). The economy is an irrevocable process of transformation of resources, as free energy, into waste which is bounded energy, continuously increasing entropy which reflects economic disorder. In this framework, maximum entropy, or maximum economic disorder, would mean the end of the economic process, since there would be no more free energy left and thereby no means to create order. When negative externalities are absent, innovation improves the economic process through the creation of order in the economic process, thus reducing the irrevocable increase of disorder. The increase of entropy decreases, thus postponing the end of the economic process.

Yet, innovation may lead to negative externalities, as Witt (1996b) argues. Consequently, Witt tries to find a social contract which may reduce the social costs of innovation and still maintain innovativeness at a high level. In my analysis, I will assume that there is a set of historically evolved conventions which provides a social selection mechanism reducing negative externalities over time. This is consistent with the view of Chang and Kozul-Wright (1994) that the national system of entrepreneurship consists of a set of institutions which, on the one hand, encourages innovation and risk-taking, but on the other hand, manages the destructive component of entrepreneurship.

In the long run, the social selection mechanism which reduces negative externalities over time assures that only quality ladders whose negative externalities are sufficiently low will survive. When innovation improves quality of the economic process along the quality ladders which are viable in the long run, the irrevocable increase of entropy, or economic disorder, decreases. Hence, the Grossman-Helpman model should be seen as quality upgrading of the economic process in the long run, when a set of conventions provides a social mechanism which selects the quality ladders whose negative externalities are sufficiently low. These conventions, thus, generate growth regimes.

In a multisector context, absolute economizing that reduces entropy growth takes place when the intermediate goods' sector differentiates its products through quality improvement, because productivity increases. Following Aghion and Howitt (1992), the consumer goods' sector becomes able to produce its goods more efficiently in terms of factor inputs. Vertical product differentiation in the consumer goods' sector, however, economizes to reduce entropy growth only in relative terms, unless the old products are immediately replaced by the old products. On the one hand, higher quality products are produced, given the factor inputs in the economic process, but on the other hand, more products are added, thus increasing the consumption of free energy.

In the Grossman-Helpman model, all goods - intermediate goods and consumer goods alike - are always of the highest extant quality. Innovation yields goods of higher quality which immediately replace the old goods which used to be of the highest quality.

Such a quality upgrading endogenous growth model is, therefore, consistent with Schumpeter's (1911) theory of economic evolution and Georgescu-Roegen's (1971) entropy interpretation thereof. Industrial innovation is an interactive process between economizing which reduces entropy growth in absolute terms through productivity improvement and economizing which reduces entropy growth in relative terms through market expansion. In the Grossman-Helpman model, market expansion means that the quality leader takes all the market immediately, thus representing a long run outcome.

What is the role of money and finance in this quality upgrading process? Money matters only in a world of uncertainty (Davidson, 1978), making imperfect information a necessary condition. When there is asymmetric information between creditors, financial institutions matter. Differences between financial systems are relevant to the analysis of real economic growth, because banks have an advantage as information producers concerning their client firms (Campbell and Kracaw, 1980, Diamond, 1984, and Fama, 1985).

Firms stay with the same bank, because high quality firms are informationally captured, as inside banks develop information inaccessible to outside banks (Sharpe, 1990). Banks may develop inside information through a low-cost ongoing history of financial information production (Fama, 1985).

This history of information production through continuous banker-entrepreneur interaction, I call learning-by-financing. Informationally captured firms and their bank form a bank-industry network, an organic institution evolving as firms become and remain informationally captured by banks. Banks have private information, while investors in corporate bonds only have public information (MacKie-Mason, 1989, and Sharpe, 1990). The private information is the result of learning-by-financing which increases the probability of a correct allocation.

In a dynamic setting, this requires that banks adapt to change in their learning-by-financing, because the continuous evolution of the economic environment influences the true entrepreneurial value of their client firms.

Previous private information may become obsolete over time. The birth and death of learning-by-financing are not considered in the extension of the Grossman-Helpman model. However, the evolutionary game-theoretic model, which I develop in chapter 4, implies that the duration of network links may lead to a high learning-by-financing initially with a possible decline over time due to negative network externalities. Nevertheless, continuous learning-by-financing yields private information. In terms of Heiner's (1988a,b) imperfect decision theory, the reliability of the banker at using appropriate information increases through learning-by-financing. A low success probability would give a high interest rate spread (Gertler, Hubbard, and Kashyap, 1991), so learning-by-financing may decrease the cost of capital for members of the bank-industry network.

The network is a device to internalize externalities for members (Teubal and Zuscovitch, 1994). A privileged group maintains its stability by producing a joint product of private and public goods (Sandler, 1992). Bank-industry networks are privileged groups where the banker's learning-by-financing concerning each individual entrepreneur benefits from the learning across all links between the banker and the set of entrepreneurs belonging to the network. The bank-industry network is, therefore, reflected in the individual links between bankers and entrepreneurs.

According to Saint-Paul (1992), there is a strategic complementarity between financial markets and technology, since financial diversification allows for hedging and thereby division of labor, thus giving technological specialization. However, the better the learning-by-financing, the higher technological risks may be taken without increasing financial fragility. Hence, the size of the quality increments, determining the entrepreneurial rent, depend on the financial system.

Section 3.2 gives the basic model which is used in section 3.3 to compare sixteen growth regimes. Section 3.4 considers quality upgrading which is endogenous to the financial system. The modified model is used in section 3.5 to compare eight growth regimes. In section 3.6, endogenous R&D productivity is brought into the analysis, giving four growth regimes. Section 3.7 deals with market entropy and the financial system as information hierarchy. Section 3.8 gives a summary.

3.2 The Basic Model: An Extension of the Grossman-Helpman Model

This section extends the quality-ladder model developed by Grossman and Helpman (1991a) with asymmetric information between creditors. Financial institutions and credit are brought into the analysis, thus introducing the financial system and some disequilibrium features in the capital market.

Learning-by-financing gives a better evaluation of the true entrepreneurial value of the firm and is represented by a parameter θ. As I will show in chapter 4, learning-by-financing is a process which depends on the duration of network links.

The quality ladder represents logarithmic quality levels of a product, lnQ. Quality improves through discrete jumps in infinite time, according to $Q_m(j) = \lambda Q_{m-1}(j)$, $\lambda > 1$, for the product generation of quality m in industry j, where λ is the quality improvement when taking a further step along the quality ladder. Setting $Q_0 = 1$, implies $Q_m = \lambda^m$. Climbing the quality ladder is a process of the economy accumulating knowledge capital. The position on the ladder is in fact a direct reflection of the value of this type of capital embodied in labor which is the only production factor.

In the R&D race along the quality ladder, the winner takes everything. This is unrealistic, but captures Schumpeter's (1911) idea of transient monopoly of entrepreneurs, while the R&D race reflects innovation reduced to routine, along the lines of Schumpeter (1942). Only the brand with the lowest quality adjusted price, p_Q, is demanded, according to the following static demand function:

$$(3.1)\quad x = 1/p_Q,$$

where x is the demand for products with the lowest quality adjusted price. This is, of course, a long run outcome.

On the supply side, industrial leaders, i.e. former entrepreneurs, live on their entrepreneurial rents and undertake no R&D in equilibrium, since it would only increase R&D costs, because there are diminishing marginal returns on entrepreneurship. All R&D is carried out by followers who place themselves one step ahead of the former leaders if they succeed. This allows for creative destruction, where the transient monopoly profits of the former leaders are eliminated by the new leaders who gain transient monopoly profits. For the followers, competition makes price equal to unit costs. Leaders are one step ahead, so all state of the art products bear the same limit price:

$$(3.2)\quad p_Q = \lambda w,$$

where w is the marginal cost of the only factor, labor.

Assuming constant returns to scale and an input-output coefficient equal to unity, yields to the leader the operational profits, $\pi = (p\text{-}w)x$, but the total costs include the cost of corporate debt, $\varphi = r\beta$, where r is the interest rate on corporate loans and $\beta \equiv B/wx$ the ratio of debt to labor (factor) costs, since the existing industry leader has benefited from credit creation to innovate. If there were increasing returns to scale, then labor costs would decrease with size, thus corresponding to higher quality increments for large firms. Similarly, decreasing returns to scale would imply lower quality increments for large firms.

The debt costs are, therefore, the price the industry-leading firm pays for its transient monopoly. For simplicity, β varies with r in such a way as to keep the debt costs, φ, constant. The entrepreneurs decide what φ to have. The owners receive the entrepreneurial rent, $\varepsilon = \pi\text{-}r\beta wx$, as dividends.

Given equations (3.1) and (3.2), the sales of the leaders, $1/\lambda w$ per unit time, yield to the owners of the industry-leading firm the corresponding flow of entrepreneurial rents:

(3.3) $\varepsilon = 1 - (1+\varphi)\delta$,

where $\delta \equiv 1/\lambda$ and $\varphi < (1 - \delta)/\delta$.

Let v denote the stock market value of the leading firm[2] in an industry, when the stock market has perfect information about the true value of the firm, ι the aggregate innovative (R&D) intensity, and 1/a the labor productivity of the R&D effort. Then, the innovative effort during the time period dt may yield v with probability ιdt at cost $wa\iota dt$, maximizing the net gain from research, $(v\iota dt\text{-}wa\iota dt)$. Hence, there is either no innovativeness, because the stock market value of the leading firm is smaller than the productivity adjusted labor costs of R&D, wa, or innovativeness is positive, because the stock market value equals the productivity adjusted labor costs of R&D. This gives the necessary free entry condition for creative destruction:

(3.4) $v \leq wa$ with equality whenever $\iota > 0$.

The value of the firm is, thus, related to the cost of market entry.

Introducing asymmetric information between financial institutions in the capital market, the distinction between private and public sources of funds becomes essential, in fact, more important than the distinction between debt and equity, because information costs matter. Private debt and equity have lower information costs than public debt and equity (MacKie-Mason, 1989).

Firms prefer better informed investors who require a lower risk premium, so asymmetric information implies a financing hierarchy (Myers, 1984) where private sources, such as retained earning and bank loans, are preferred to the more costly public sources, like bonds, CPs, and new equity share issues.

The financial system in my extension of the Grossman-Helpman model is organized in such a way as to finance innovation through debt, borrowing either privately, bank credit, or publicly, corporate bonds. When becoming the new leader, the successful entrepreneur turns some of the accumulated debt into equity. Grossman and Helpman (1991a) used equity issues as the only source of finance.

Hence, the financing hierarchy consists of two levels, private funds and public funds.[3] Let innovation be financed by debt, while equity is traded in a secondary market, the stock price functioning as an indicator for investors what interest rate to demand on corporate bonds. Investors are assumed to demand the same return on corporate bonds as corporate stock, since they keep efficient portfolios.

McCauley and Zimmer (1989) find empirically that close bank-industry links provide risk spreading so that leveraging lowers the cost of capital. According to Becchetti (1995), the cost differentials between internal and external financing appears to be small in Japan, where the strong bank-industry links give extensive formal and informal monitoring. The banks are considerably more well informed than other investors, making bank credit much more advantageous than corporate bonds. In addition, bank loans give the stock market a noisy signal of the true value of firms. James (1987) finds that new bank credit has larger positive effect on the stock prices than new public debt issues.

Hence, learning-by-financing may be formalized by letting network banks provide a perfect signal concerning the true firm value of network firms, reflecting fundamentals, while independent banks only provide a noisy signal. Sharpe (1990) uses a similar approach in his comparison of inside and outside banks.

The firm value of an industry leader is v, but if an entrepreneur succeeds in innovating, this value is lost through creative destruction. Let $\gamma \in \{v,0\}$ be the perfect signal of firm value, available to network banks, and

$\tilde{\gamma} \epsilon \{\tilde{v}, \tilde{0}\}$ the noisy signal, available to capital market investors, with the distribution function:

$$\text{prob}(\tilde{\gamma}=\tilde{v} \mid v) = \frac{1+\theta}{2} \quad (3.5)$$

$$\text{prob}(\tilde{\gamma}=\tilde{v} \mid 0) = \frac{1-\theta}{2}$$

where $0 \leq \theta \leq 1$ is the learning-by-financing coefficient and the probabilities are the probability of a noisy signal of firm value v when this is the true value and the probability of a firm value v when the true value is 0, respectively. Perfect learning-by-financing implies $\theta=1$. Using Heiner's (1988a,b) terminology, this corresponds to an infinite reliability of the banker at using information.

In general, the closer the bank-industry links are, the larger the impact of bank learning-by-financing is. The finite reliability of the banker at using information increases. Here, the learning-by-financing of the bank within a bank-industry network is taken as numeraire. A network bank's learning-by-financing is, thus, assumed to be perfect. Both the firm value of the extant leader, v, and the R&D productivity of entrepreneurs at perfect allocation, 1/a, are correctly estimated at the stock market by the signal from the bank. Arm's length distance between banks and industry, however, turns bankers into market investors.

Corresponding to Zysman's (1983) differences in banking behavior between credit- and market-based financial systems,[4] I let the imperfectly informed arm's length banker overestimate the value of the extant leader who has proven his leadership by past performance. The reason is the imperfect allocation of funds of the arm's length banker, which decreases the R&D productivity of the entrepreneurs.

The imperfect allocation of funds causes, through equation (3.4), an overestimation of the value of extant leaders. Naturally, the R&D productivity depends on the probability of the noisy signal being correct, as given by equation (3.5). At the stock market, the higher the bank learning-by-financing, the more reliable signal the stock market will receive concerning the R&D productivity of the entrepreneurs. Consequently, the firm value of extant leaders decreases with bank learning-by-financing:

$$(3.6)\quad v_m = \frac{2v}{1+\theta} \leq wa_m = \frac{2wa}{1+\theta} \text{ with equality whenever } \iota > 0,$$

where v_m is the stock market value of a leading firm and $1/a_m$ the labor productivity of R&D.

The cost of knowledge capital required to innovate will increase as imperfect allocation increases entry costs. In other words, the cost of knowledge capital depends on the elasticity of the corporate interest rate with respect to the variation of the stock market value of extant leaders, thus giving an interest rate spread, S. Let ζ denote this elasticity where the inverse of the probability of the noisy signal of firm value being true is the inverse of the probability of the good state. Since ρ is the riskfree interest rate on corporate debt, $\zeta = (S/\rho)(1+\theta)/(1-\theta)$.[5]

In the organized capital market as institution converting uncertainty into subjective risk, the internal structure may be such that market investors have routines which give them a high reliability at responding to signals from the bankers, so they keep their portfolios close to efficient. Groups of traders may create stability through a high density of interaction (Mizruchi and Brewster Stearns, 1994). Following Heiner (1988a), they may delay adjustments, because there are adjustment costs. This gives a higher reliability than immediate responses and thereby a higher capacity of keeping portfolios close to efficient.

Let us then assume that capital market agents keep their portfolios efficient, making $\zeta=1$. Hence, the cost of entrepreneurial knowledge capital, i.e. the cost of debt, increases in percent as much as the stock market value of the extant leader. Differences between financial systems in the cost of knowledge capital arise, because stronger bank-industry networks yield a higher probability that the noisy signal is correct through a higher learning-by-financing, θ.

What matters, however, is *not* whether the banks or the market provide the funds, but whether the bank-industry networks are sufficiently strong to make the banks efficient information producers in the capital market. Thus, in a mixed financial system, industrial finance by securities directly in the market becomes cheaper if there are strong bank-industry networks so information production may be delegated to the banks.[6]

Information production by banks will influence the shareholders' rate of return through an adjustment of the creative destruction and asymmetric information risks. The creative destruction risk is given by the aggregate innovative intensity, ι. Hence, the probability that one of these efforts targeted at taking over the industry-leader's transient monopoly profits succeeds is equal to ιdt. The expected rate of return for shareholders in an industry-leading firm becomes $(\varepsilon + \dot{v} - \iota v)dt$, where ε is the entrepreneurial rent as dividend, $\dot{v}$ is a capital gain on shareholding, and ιv is the cost of creative destruction. Consider the case of symmetric information. This implies that the stock owners hold a well diversified portfolio, where the return on stock ownership would have been equal to the interest rate on riskfree bonds. The latter are riskfree assets, because neither creative destruction risks nor asymmetric information risks influence them. The riskfree interest rate is the zero inflation interest rate of the economy, since there is no inflation in the model. The liquidity of the economy, therefore, yields economic growth without inflation for the riskfree interest rate at issue.

As information is asymmetric in the capital markets, there will be a disequilibrium gap between the firms' marginal cost of finance and the riskfree interest rate, ρ, covered by the spread, S:

$$(3.7)\quad \varepsilon + \dot{v}_m - \iota v_m = (\rho + S)v_m,$$

where $S > 0$ whenever $v_m > v$ and $S = 0$ whenever $v_m = v$. Since $\zeta = 1$ with efficient portfolios, uncertainty is reflected in the spread, $S = (v_m - v)\rho / v$. Hence, the spread is given by:

$$(3.8)\quad S = \frac{1 - \theta}{1 + \theta}\rho.$$

Equations (3.3) and (3.7) and definition $V \equiv 1/v_m$ give a differential equation for the inverse firm value:

$$(3.9)\quad \frac{\dot{V}}{V} = (1 - (1+\varphi)\delta)V - \iota - \rho - S.$$

Setting $\dot{V} = 0$, thus making the extant leader's cost of equity increase with aggregate innovative intensity, gives the VV curve:

$$(3.10)\quad V = \frac{\iota + \rho + S}{1 - (1+\varphi)\delta}$$

In the labor market, total labor supply, L, is kept constant to minimize the entropy increase, while on the demand side, $a\iota$ is employment in R&D with $(1+\varphi)\delta/w$ being employment in manufacturing.

Credit has given the entrepreneurs the required purchasing power to innovate, but the interest payments to the creditors constitute an additional production cost. An additional loan increases φ, so δ has to decrease to keep the entrepreneurial rent constant, according to equation (3.3). Unless this condition is fulfilled, an additional loan would increase manufacturing employment, thus decreasing the labor supply available to R&D. This requires an increase in the labor productivity in R&D, just to maintain innovativeness, since the labor market always clears, according to the full employment condition:

$$(3.11)\quad a_m\iota + \frac{(1+\varphi)\delta}{w} = L,$$

where the equilibrium wage is fixed by negotiation in such a way as to keep $wL \geq (1+\varphi)\delta$ in order to assure a nonnegative R&D employment. Full employment is consistent with Schumpeter (1911), because the allocation of labor between production and innovative efforts takes place within the circular flow which is characterized by full employment.

One could, however, bring in unemployment into the model as a reduction of total labor supply actually employed, i.e. a lower L. This would give a lower R&D productivity of the economy at perfect resource allocation, L/a, which is the ratio of innovativeness to the share of total labor supply employed in R&D. Hence, unemployment would be equal to a lower labor productivity of the R&D effort at full employment. The full-employment condition (3.11) and the adjusted creative destruction condition (3.6) give the LL curve:

$$(3.12)\quad \iota = \begin{cases} \dfrac{(1+\theta)L}{2a} - (1+\varphi)\delta V \text{ for } V < \dfrac{(1+\theta)L}{(1+\varphi)2a\delta}, \\ 0 \text{ otherwise.} \end{cases}$$

Substituting equation (3.8) into equation (3.10) yields a spread-adjusted VV curve which is dependent on the extent of economy-wide bank learning-by-financing. At its intersection with the LL curve, from equation (3.12), the economy is in a steady state dynamic equilibrium:

$$(3.13a)\quad \iota^* = (1 - (1+\varphi)\delta)\frac{(1+\theta)L}{2a} - (\frac{1-\theta}{1+\theta}+1)(1+\varphi)\delta\rho$$

$$(3.13b)\quad V^* = \frac{(1+\theta)L}{2a} + (\frac{1-\theta}{1+\theta}+1)\rho.$$

The economy is assumed to jump immediately to this steady state dynamic equilibrium, (ι^*,V^*). At equilibrium, the impact of asymmetric information at the capital markets is obvious, since the spread becomes positive and increases with the information asymmetry.

As equations (3.13a,b) show, bank learning-by-financing increases the aggregate innovative intensity, but also the inverse stock market value as long as the better R&D resource allocation is more effective than the interest rate. We have, thus, seen how a financial system with strong bank-industry networks may increase the aggregate innovative intensity in the economy through learning-by-financing, but what are the links to growth and entropy?

Bankers and entrepreneurs are unaware of the arrival rate of innovations, but in order to study the links between innovation and economic evolution, one may assume that the arrival rate is a Poisson process. Considering the arrival rate of innovations as a Poisson process and using the law of large numbers, Grossman and Helpman (1991a) show how innovation at the aggregate level is smooth and stable, so that the expected number of products (or processes) upgraded are ιt. The distribution of product qualities evolve within and across industries, implying a constant growth rate g_D of the representative consumer's instantaneous utility ln D(t) where ιt represents quality and equations (3.1) and (3.2) demand:

$$(3.14)\quad ln D(t) = \iota t ln\lambda - ln w - ln\lambda,$$

whose time derivative gives the quality-based growth rate:

$$(3.15)\quad g_D = \iota ln\lambda.$$

Note that the representative consumer's instantaneous utility grows at the constant rate g_D, while consumer spending, being the numeraire, remains constant. Hence, the growth rate g_D represents purely qualitative growth being the difference between the growth of consumer utility and the growth of entropy. The utility-entropy gap becomes continuously larger over time. This implies continuously decreasing marginal costs of quality-based utility to the consumers.

A financial system with strong bank-industry networks allowing for efficient learning-by-financing, decreases the spread and thereby the costs of financing innovation, increasing innovation and quality-based growth through a faster growing utility-entropy gap.

3.3 Innovation and Differences between Financial Systems in Costs of Knowledge Capital: Simulation Results with Sixteen Equilibrium Regimes

Institutional differences in the financial system and the industrial structure between growth regimes give multiple equilibria. The basic model may be used to compare different dynamic equilibria, as outcomes of various combinations of financial systems and industrial structures.

In order to analyze the interaction between the variables determining a dynamic equilibrium, I have made simulations for sixteen growth regimes, each one having its own specific dynamic equilibrium. Each regime consists of two financial (monetary), and two real variables, the two financial ones being learning-by-financing, θ, and the riskfree interest rate, ρ, which is interpreted as the return on a portfolio of riskfree securities.

Such an analysis will allow for an analysis of the compatibility of financial and industrial innovation,[7] since financial innovation makes ρ higher. According to equation (3.7) of the basic model, the required rate of return on industrial innovation increases, but the banks as information producers influence the rate of return requirement.

In my model, strong bank-industry networks decrease the costs of knowledge capital, because the learning-by-financing efficiency is higher when the bank-industry networks are strong, thus increasing aggregate innovative intensity. A financial system with strong bank-industry networks is characterized by a higher θ.

This implies a lower spread which decreases the rate of return requirement, according to equations (3.7) and (3.8). Therefore, my model predicts a lower spread for bank-industry networks, i.e. lower subjective risk premia on the corporate interest rate, which will increase the aggregate innovative intensity (R&D targeted at destroying the extant leader), ι, through lower rate of return requirements on industrial innovation.

The two real variables are the product of the R&D productivity of the economy at perfect resource allocation, L/a, i.e. the ratio of innovativeness to the share of total labor supply which is allocated to R&D,[8] and the inverse of the size of the quality ladder steps, δ. The smaller δ is, the higher the quality improvements due to innovation are, yielding larger entrepreneurial rents. The other side of the coin is that larger quality improvements require more knowledge capital which in turn demands more R&D to destroy the transient monopoly of the extant leader in the industry. The higher the labor productivity in R&D, i.e. the higher the L/a, the lower the entry costs becomes, thus increasing the degree of competition by lowering the competence/difficulty gap. Following Heiner (1988a,b), the reliability at using information becomes higher and a greater number of entrepreneurs fulfill the minimum requirement, thus increasing entry into the market.

Hence, a growth regime is a binary quadruple, $[\theta,\rho,(L/a),\delta]$, where each variable has a low value denoted by 0 and a high one denoted by 1. This gives sixteen growth regimes composed of four monetary (financial) subregimes and four real (techno-organizational) subregimes.

The monetary subregime consists of a financial system with high and low learning-by-financing, each being exposed to high and low returns on a riskfree portfolio of securities. The real subregime involves high and low R&D competence, i.e. R&D productivity of the economy at perfect resource allocation, exposed to a high or low R&D difficulty, i.e. quality increments which determine the transient monopoly profits. In the simulations, the low and high values of the four exogenous variables are set to:

(i) θ: 0.0 and 1.0,
(ii) ρ: 0.02 and 0.04,
(iii) L/a: 0.85 and 1.0,
(iv) δ: 0.67 and 0.72.

In all simulations φ=0.16, making the entrepreneurs' decision rules equal between financial systems. The simulation results in sixteen dynamic steady state equilibria, one for each of the sixteen growth regimes, illustrated in Figure 3.1.

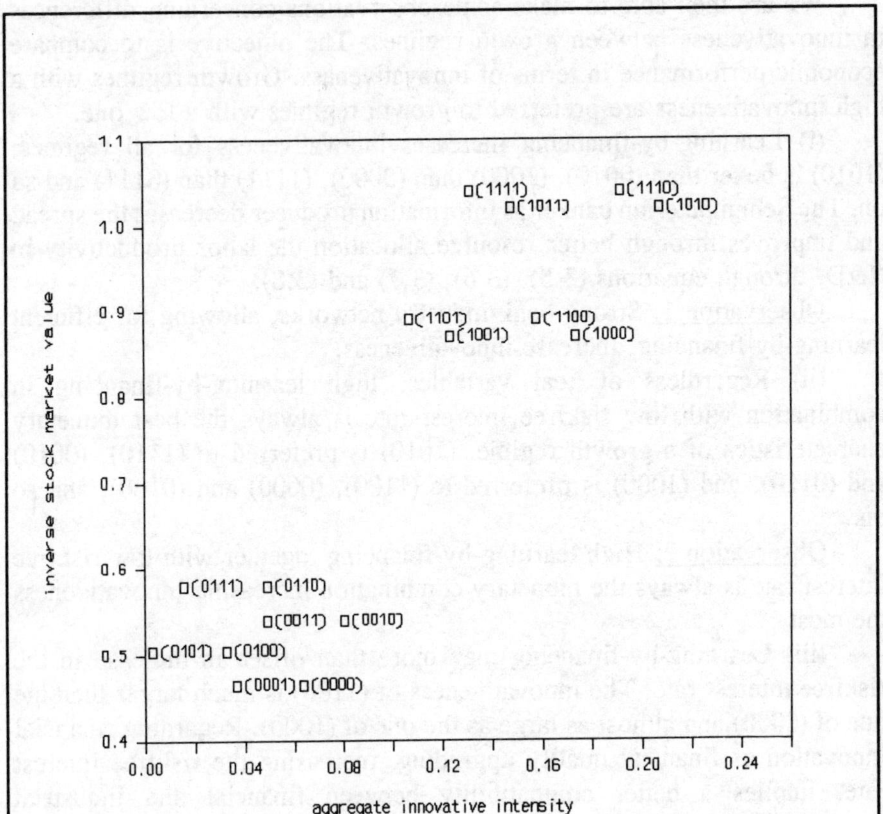
1.1
1.0
0.9
0.8
0.7
0.6
0.5
0.4
inverse stock market value
(1111)
(1110)
(1011)
(1010)
(1101)
(1001)
(1100)
(1000)
(0111)
(0110)
(0011)
(0010)
(0101)
(0100)
(0001)
(0000)
0.00
0.04
0.08
0.12
0.16
0.20
0.24
aggregate innovative intensity

Figure 3.1

We are then able to make some observations concerning differences in innovativeness between growth regimes. The objective is to compare economic performance in terms of innovativeness. Growth regimes with a high innovativeness are preferred to growth regimes with a low one.

(i) Learning-by-financing increases innovativeness for all regimes; (1010) is better than (0010), (1000) than (0000), (1111) than (0111) and so on. The Schumpeterian banker as information producer decreases the spread and improves through better resource allocation the labor productivity in R&D, through equations (3.5), (3.6), (3,7) and (3.8).

Observation 1: Strong bank-industry networks, allowing for efficient learning-by-financing, increase innovativeness.

(ii) Regardless of real variables, high learning-by-financing in combination with low riskfree interest rate is always the best monetary characteristics of a growth regime. (1010) is preferred to (1110), (0010) and (0110), and (1000) is preferred to (1100), (0000) and (0100), and so on.

Observation 2: High learning-by-financing together with low riskfree interest rate is always the monetary combination increasing innovativeness the most.

(iii) Learning-by-financing may more than offset an increase in the riskfree interest rate. The innovativeness of (1100) is much larger than the one of (0000) and almost as large as the one of (1000). Regarding financial innovation as financial quality upgrading, increasing the riskfree interest rate, implies a better compatibility between financial and industrial innovation, resolving the Minsky's incompatibility problem between financial and industrial innovation.

Observation 3: Learning-by-financing may resolve Minsky's incompatibility problem between financial and industrial innovation.

(iv) Innovativeness increases when the R&D productivity of the economy at perfect resource allocation is high, as an outcome of the full employment condition, equation (3.11). For example, (0010) is preferred to (0000). A high R&D productivity decreases the entry and exit costs, wa and v respectively in equation (3.3). This is consistent with the empirical findings of international innovativeness differences (Ergas, 1985).

Observation 4: Innovativeness increases when entrepreneurial exit and entry costs are low.

(v) The higher the quality improvements, i.e. the lower the δ, the higher innovativeness becomes. The best regime (1010) is preferred to

(1011). The explanation is to be found in equation (3.3). Since the ratio of debt to operational costs is constant, the lower the δ, the higher are the entrepreneurial rents, the very incentive for a Schumpeterian entrepreneur.

Observation 5: High entrepreneurial rents give a high innovativeness.

(vi) There are diminishing marginal returns of either increasing labor productivity in R&D or the quality increments. Starting in (1001), an increase in L/a would move the economy to (1011), while a decrease in δ would move the economy from (1001) to (1000), both of which are much worse than (1010), where the two adjustments have been combined. In the former case, the entry costs are low, but the entrepreneurial rents are low as well. Competition is too strong, because the high aggregate innovative competence, given by L/a, is wasted on projects with a too low innovative difficulty, given by δ.[9] In the latter case, a decrease in δ, increasing the innovative difficulty, would for a low R&D productivity, keeping L/a low, imply too high entry costs. Consequently, the extant leader may enjoy high entrepreneurial rent at a low risk of creative destruction. In this case, innovativeness suffers, because industrial structure is too monopolistic.

Observation 6: A high R&D competence, a high R&D productivity yielding low entry costs, have to be combined with a high R&D difficulty, high quality increments yielding high entrepreneurial rents. Competition has to be strong, but must not wipe out the transient monopoly profits necessary for entrepreneurs to have an incentive to innovate.[10]

Hence, endogenizing the real variables to the monetary ones requires that learning-by-financing, through the spread, increases labor productivity in R&D, 1/a, and the quality increments, $\lambda \equiv 1/\delta$.

3.4 Endogenous Quality Upgrading and the Financial System: A Further Extension of the Grossman-Helpman Model

Grossman and Helpman (1991a) make quality upgrading endogenous by allowing firms to choose their quality increments. I let the entrepreneurs choose the ratio of debt costs to factor (labor) costs rather than the quality increment. As Amendola and Gaffard (1988) point out, financial constraints as well as human constraints influence innovation. Consequently, debt finance lifts the financial constraint, thus decreasing δ down to the point where the human constraint imposes a limit. Hence, there is a potential δ which may be reached by debt finance. Let us assume entrepreneurs have a decision rule which is sophisticated enough to maximize the stockholders' utility of innovation by adopting φ to reach this potential δ.[11]

How does the financial system manage to fulfill the interests of the stockholders of the firms? A higher λ makes the economic process more efficient, but is achieved through high R&D productivity in order to maintain a high innovativeness. Only then, the new, more efficient, economic process diffuses.

Hence, an efficient combination of φ and λ has to be chosen. The former is given by the entrepreneur's decision rule, while the latter is set by the financial system, because improvements in the labor productivity of R&D, 1/a, are made possible through credit.

Let us assume that the entrepreneur uses corporate debt to innovate, given the value of λ allowed for by the financial system, in such a way that the shareholders' net benefit from R&D, $\iota v(\lambda)dt - \iota wa(\lambda)dt$, is maximized. Here, $\iota v(\lambda)dt$ is the benefit of innovation at intensity ι during period dt and $\iota wa(\lambda)dt$ the corresponding costs. Hence, the entrepreneur's decision rule satisfies:

$$(3.16)\ v'(\lambda) = wa'(\lambda).$$

Following equation (3.4), the value of the firm equals the cost of innovation, so the entrepreneur's borrowing decision holds for any aggregate innovative intensity, because there are no net benefits of R&D to the individual entrepreneur.

Assume ι, ϵ, ρ, S, and v to be constant over time, so equations (3.3), (3.4), and (3.7) imply that the firm value equals its stream of expected entrepreneurial rents discounted by the sum of the innovativeness, ι, and the corporate interest rate, $\rho+S$:

$$(3.17)\ wa(\lambda) = v(\lambda) = \frac{1 - \dfrac{1+\varphi}{\lambda}}{\iota+\rho+S}.$$

Equation (3.17) and its derivative, $v'(\lambda)$, together with (3.16), give the increment of R&D resource requirements to achieve the quality increment made possible by the financial system:

$$(3.18)\ \frac{\lambda a'(\lambda)}{a(\lambda)} = \frac{1+\varphi}{\lambda - (1+\varphi)},$$

where the expression on the left of the equality sign is the elasticity of R&D resource requirements, i.e. entry costs, with respect to quality increments. This elasticity is always positive, but the higher its value, the higher the R&D resource requirements to realize the given quality increment. The Schumpeterian banker provides the entrepreneur with sufficient purchasing power through credit creation which decreases the gap between actual and potential R&D productivity. Hence, the elasticity of R&D resource requirements with respect to quality increments should be negatively correlated with borrowing, because the financial constraint is taken away, but as borrowing increases the human constraint becomes more apparent. The two constraints are represented as a logarithmic increase of quality increments for a given input increase of R&D resources when borrowing increases. Hence, the inverse elasticity is supposed to increase logarithmically with borrowing, $b_0+b_1 ln\beta$, giving the following expression:

$$(3.19)\quad \frac{\lambda a'(\lambda)}{a(\lambda)} = \frac{1}{b_0+b_1(ln\varphi - ln(\rho+S))}.$$

Equations (3.18) and (3.19) give the unique λ allowed for by the financial system, maximizing stockholders utility:

$$(3.20)\quad \lambda = (b_0+b_1(ln\varphi - ln(\rho+S))+1)(1+\varphi).$$

Hence, quality upgrading has become endogenized. The quality increments increase with corporate borrowing. In other words, the entrepreneur may introduce more radical innovations when the banker supplies more purchasing power.

3.5 Endogenous Quality Upgrading and Differences in the Costs of Knowledge Capital: Simulation Results with Eight Equilibrium Regimes

In this simulation round, a growth regime is reduced to a binary triple, $[\theta,\rho,(L/a)]$, because δ is determined through equation (3.20). Innovation has two constraints, the financial one and the human one (Amendola and Gaffard, 1988). The financial constraint is given by the learning-by-financing and the riskfree interest rate, the two variables which in turn determines the size of the quality increments, while the human one by the R&D productivity for a given total labor supply.

For financial markets without financial intermediation, Saint-Paul (1992) shows how financial diversification leads to higher productivity and growth by allowing for technological specialization. In this study where banks exist and bank-industry networks are possible, the distinction is not between technological and financial equilibrium, but between a high bank credit financial equilibrium characterized by financial specialization in a bank-industry network, on the one hand, and a low corporate bond financial equilibrium characterized by financial diversification due to arm's length finance, on the other hand.

Let us turn to the model to see that learning-by-financing opens up for another approach than financial diversification. In a dynamic equilibrium which is an outcome of a financial system without any learning-by-financing, $\theta=0$, capital market uncertainty prevails, i.e. creditors do not know what entrepreneurs to give credit to, so they diversify their portfolios. When learning-by-financing is perfect, $\theta=1$, the banks have perfect knowledge about entrepreneurs due to close bank-industry links. Perfect learning-by-financing implies a capital market characterized by certainty, so the capital market supplies more and cheaper credit, because full financial specialization within a bank-industry network is possible.

L/a is the only real variable, so there are two sets of financial equilibria, given the human constraint: (i) (000), (010), (100), and (110), for L/a low, and (ii) (001), (011), (101), and (111), for L/a high.

In the simulations, $\varphi=0.16$, $b_0=0.2$, and $b_1=0.05$. The low and high values of the three exogenous variables are set to:
(i) θ: 0.0 and 1.0,
(ii) ρ: 0.02 and 0.04,
(iii) L/a: 0.85 and 1.0.

3.5.1 Simulation Results with Eight Growth Regimes

The eight different dynamic equilibria of this simulation round are shown in Figure 3.2.

(vii) Grouping equilibria according to learning-by-financing gives the outcome that (101), (100), (111), and (110) perform better than (001), (000), (011), and (010).

<u>Observation 7:</u> A high learning-by-financing decreases the financial constraints to innovation compared to the low learning-by-financing by allowing for higher quality increments.

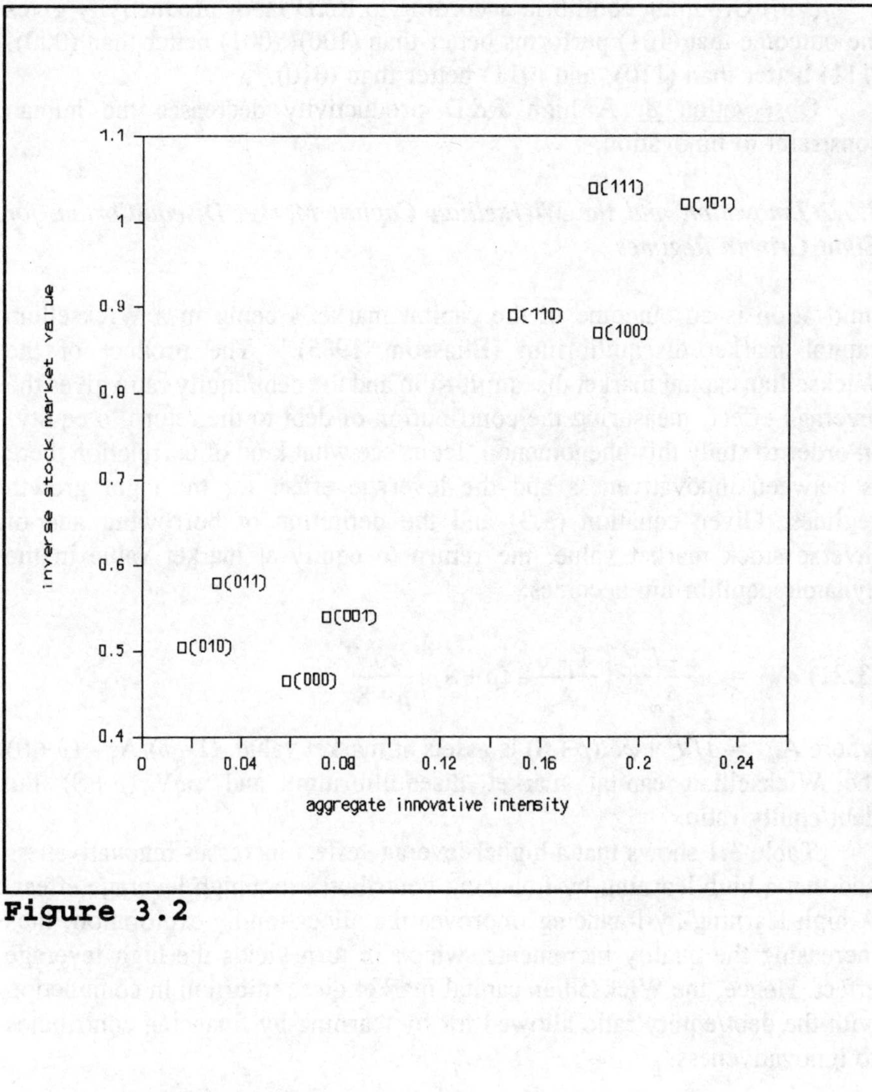
inverse stock market value
aggregate innovative intensity
1.1
1
0.9
0.8
0.7
0.6
0.5
0.4
0
0.04
0.08
0.12
0.16
0.2
0.24
(111)
(101)
(110)
(100)
(011)
(001)
(010)
(000)

Figure 3.2

(viii) Grouping equilibria according to R&D labor productivity gives the outcome that (101) performs better than (100), (001) better than (000), (111) better than (110), and (011) better than (010).

Observation 8: A high R&D productivity decreases the human constraint to innovation.

3.5.2 Innovation and the Wicksellian Capital Market Disequilibrium for Eight Growth Regimes

Innovation is an outcome of the capital market's being in a Wicksellian capital market disequilibrium (Eliasson, 1985).[12] The product of the Wicksellian capital market disequilibrium and the debt/equity ratio gives the leverage effect, measuring the contribution of debt to the return to equity. In order to study this phenomenon, let us see what kind of correlation there is between innovativeness and the leverage effect for the eight growth regimes. Given equation (3.3) and the definition of borrowing and of inverse stock market value, the return to equity at market value in the dynamic equilibrium becomes:

$$(3.21)\ \epsilon V^* = \frac{1-\delta}{A_m} + \left(\frac{1-\delta}{A_m} - (\rho+S)\right)\frac{\varphi\delta V^*}{\rho+S}$$

where $A_m = 1/V^* + \varphi\delta/(\rho+S)$ is assets at market value, $(1-\delta)/A_m - (\rho+S)$ the Wicksellian capital market disequilibrium, and $\varphi\delta V^*/(\rho+S)$ the debt/equity ratio.

Table 3.1 shows that a higher leverage effect increases innovativeness and that a high learning-by-financing contributes to a high leverage effect. A high learning-by-financing improves the allocation-by-exploration, thus increasing the quality increments, which in turn yields the high leverage effect. Hence, the Wicksellian capital market disequilibrium in conjunction with the debt/equity ratio allowed for by learning-by-financing contributes to innovativeness.

Table 3.1 Innovativeness, Return to Equity, and Leverage Effect for Eight Growth Regimes

Regime	Aggregate Innovative Intensity	Return to Equity	Leverage Effect
101	0.218	0.238	0.184
100	0.183	0.203	0.150
111	0.181	0.221	0.133
110	0.149	0.189	0.105
001	0.075	0.115	0.044
000	0.059	0.099	0.033
011	0.030	0.110	0.014
010	0.016	0.096	0.007

3.6 Endogenous Quality Upgrading and R&D Productivity: Simulation Results with Four Equilibrium Regimes

According to Amendola and Gaffard (1988), innovation has a financial constraint and a human constraint. The economy's human constraint is given by the product of total labor supply and R&D productivity in making quality increments. The elasticity of R&D productivity with respect to quality increments is the negation of the elasticity, in equation (3.19), of R&D resource requirements with respect to quality increments, giving the following human constraint elasticity:

$$(3.22)\quad \frac{\lambda L/a'(\lambda)}{L/a(\lambda)} = - \frac{\lambda a'(\lambda)}{a(\lambda)} .$$

Using equations (3.19) and (3.22), the percentage decline in R&D productivity due to an increase in quality increments can be calculated. Let $\underline{r}$ denote the lowest corporate interest rate, i.e. the lowest cost of knowledge capital, and $L/a(\lambda,\underline{r})$ the human constraint to innovation for a growth regime with the lowest cost of knowledge capital. This growth regime would have the highest quality increments, but the higher the quality increments, the lower the R&D productivity becomes. However, less tight financial constraints may increase R&D productivity for a given size of the quality increments:

$$(3.23)\ L/a = \frac{L/a(\lambda,\underline{r})}{1 - \dfrac{(ln(\rho+S) - ln\underline{r})(1+\varphi)b_1\delta}{b_0+b_1(ln\varphi - ln(\rho+S))}}.$$

In this simulation round the growth regimes are binary doubles, $[\theta,\rho]$, so we have four regimes to consider. In the simulations, $\varphi=0.16$, $b_0=0.2$, $b_1=0.05$, $L/a(\lambda,\underline{r})=0.85$, and $\underline{r}=0.02$ are equal for all regimes. The low and high values of the two exogenous variables are set to:
(i) θ: 0.0 and 1.0,
(ii) ρ: 0.02 and 0.04.

3.6.1 Simulation Results with Four Growth Regimes

The results for the four-regime case are given in Figure 3.3, giving an additional observation.

(ix) In terms of innovativeness, the best regime is (10) followed in turn by (11), (00), and (01). Regimes with a high learning-by-financing (10) and (11) give significantly higher innovativeness, while differences in riskfree interest have a very small impact on innovativeness.

Observation 9: Learning-by-financing improves the R&D productivity through a better resource allocation as well as a less tight financial constraint, allowing higher quality increments. A high riskfree interest rate makes the financial constraint tighter, thus decreasing the size of the quality increments, while leaving resource allocation unchanged.

3.6.2 Innovation and the Wicksellian Capital Market Disequilibrium for Four Growth Regimes

Table 3.2 shows for four regimes that a higher leverage effect increases innovativeness and that a high learning-by-financing contributes to a high leverage effect.

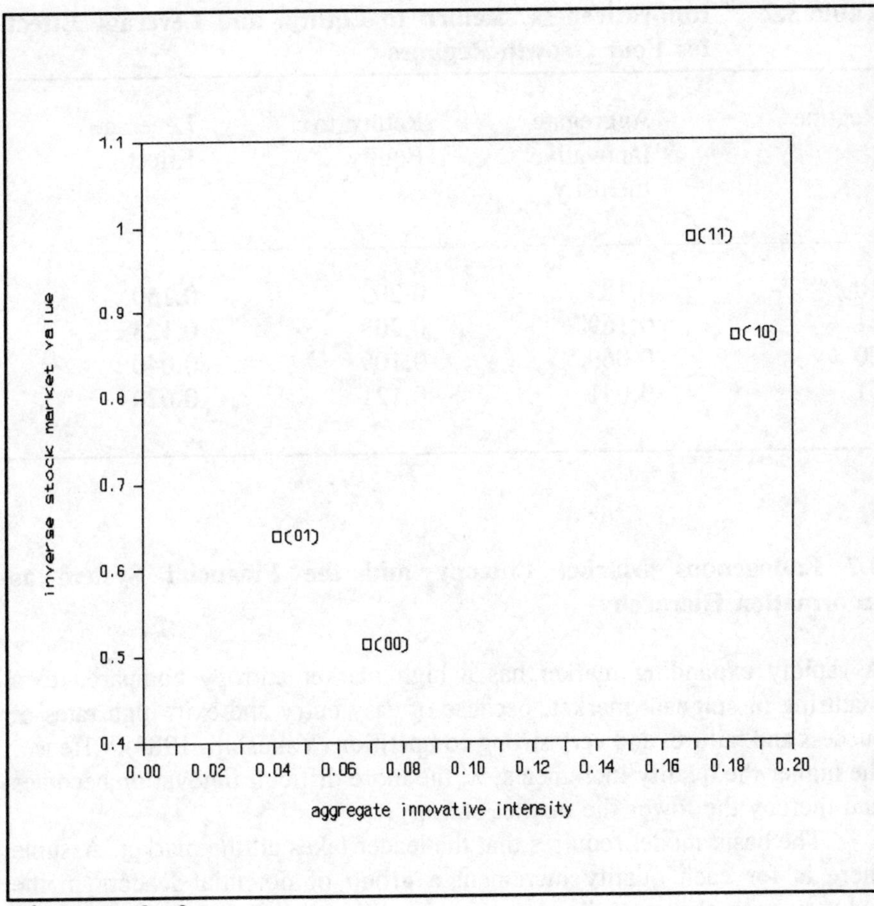
1.1
1
0.9
0.8
0.7
0.6
0.5
0.4
inverse stock market value
□(11)
□(10)
□(01)
□(00)
0.00
0.02
0.04
0.06
0.08
0.10
0.12
0.14
0.16
0.18
0.20
aggregate innovative intensity

Figure 3.3

Table 3.2 Innovativeness, Return to Equity, and Leverage Effect for Four Growth Regimes

Regime	Aggregate Innovative Intensity	Return to Equity	Leverage Effect
10	0.183	0.203	0.150
11	0.169	0.209	0.123
00	0.069	0.109	0.040
01	0.041	0.121	0.020

3.7 Endogenous Market Entropy and the Financial System as Information Hierarchy

A rapidly expanding market has a high market entropy compared to a maturing or stagnant market, because of easy entry and exit, high rates of success and failure, and very strong competition (Yakushiji, 1984).[13] Hence, the higher the quality increments, λ, the more difficult innovation becomes and thereby the lower the market entropy.

The basic model requires that the leader takes all the market. Assume there is for each quality increment a group of potential leaders in the industry with the same innovation probability, swapping the position as monopolist between themselves, and uneven innovativeness, so the number of potential leaders decreases with higher quality increments.

Then, the average market share of any potential leader is 1/n, yielding the market entropy:

(3.24) $H = - \mathit{ln}\,(1/n) = \mathit{ln}\,n.$

where n is the number of potential leaders in the industry:

(3.25) $n = y - z\lambda.$

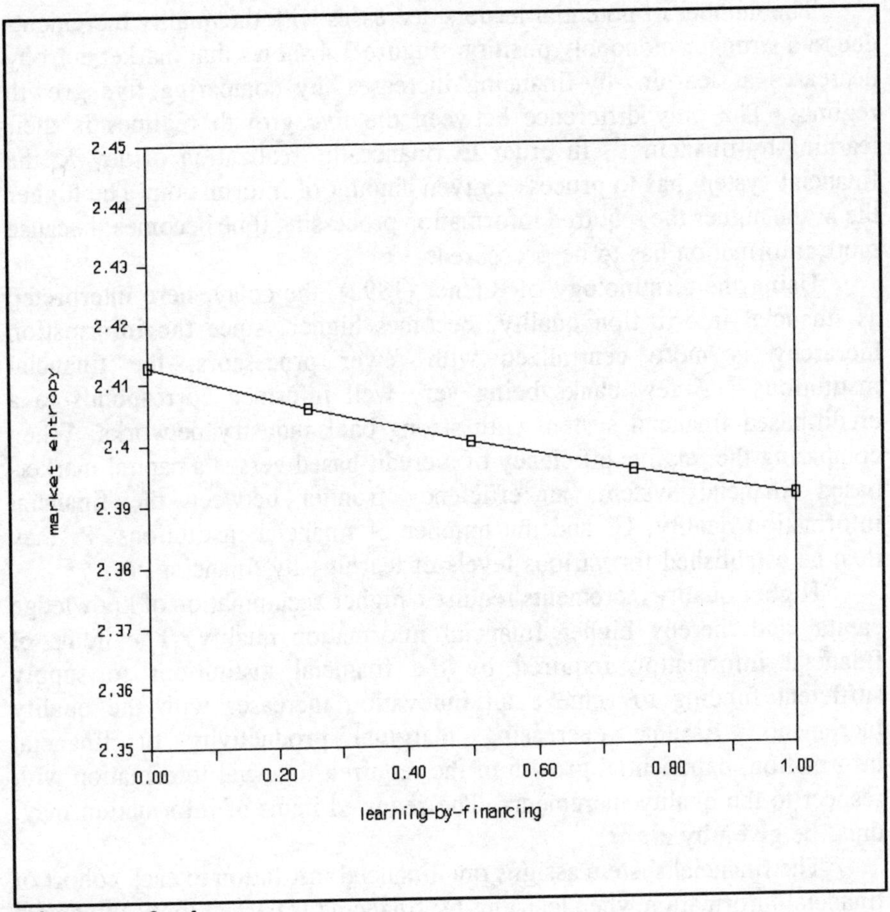
2.45
2.44
2.43
2.42
2.41
2.4
2.39
2.38
2.37
2.36
2.35
market entropy
0.00
0.20
0.40
0.60
0.80
1.00
learning-by-financing

Figure 3.4

The number of potential leaders decreases with the quality increments due to a stronger monopoly position. Figure 3.4 shows that market entropy decreases as learning-by-financing increases, by comparing five growth regimes. The only difference between the five growth regimes is their learning-by-financing.[14] In order to finance the realization of any λ, the financial system has to process a given amount of information. The higher the λ, the higher the required information processing time becomes, because more information has to be processed.

Using the terminology of Radner (1992), the delay, here interpreted as financial information quality, becomes higher, since the information hierarchy is more centralized with fewer processors, the financial institutions.[15] A few banks being very well informed corresponds to a credit-based financial system with strong bank-industry networks. When comparing the relative efficiency of a credit-based versus a capital market-based financial system, an efficiency frontier between the financial information quality, C, and the number of financial institutions, P, may then be established for various levels of learning-by-financing, θ.

Higher quality increments require a higher accumulation of knowledge capital and thereby higher financial information quality. The items of financial information required by the financial institutions to supply sufficient funding to achieve an innovation increases with the quality increments. Assume decreasing marginal productivity of financial information, exponential growth of the required financial information with respect to the quality increments. The required items of information may, thus, be given by e^{λ}.

The financial system assigns one financial institution to each cohort of financial information when learning-by-financing is perfect, but e^{λ} financial institutions, i.e. one per item, when there is no learning-by-financing. The number of financial institutions assigned to each cohort of information is, therefore, $\theta+(1-\theta)e^{\lambda}$.

As T is the arrival time for a new cohort of information, the arrival speed becomes 1/T. The higher this speed, the closer market entropy will be to its maximum, H_{max}, the market entropy when all firms are potential leaders, so $H = H_{max}(1 - e^{-1/T})$.

The cohort arrival speed, therefore, is $1/T = -\,ln(1 - H/H_{max})$. Following Radner (1992), a lower bound for pairs of financial information quality, C, and financial institutions, P, may now be calculated, giving the financial information quality:

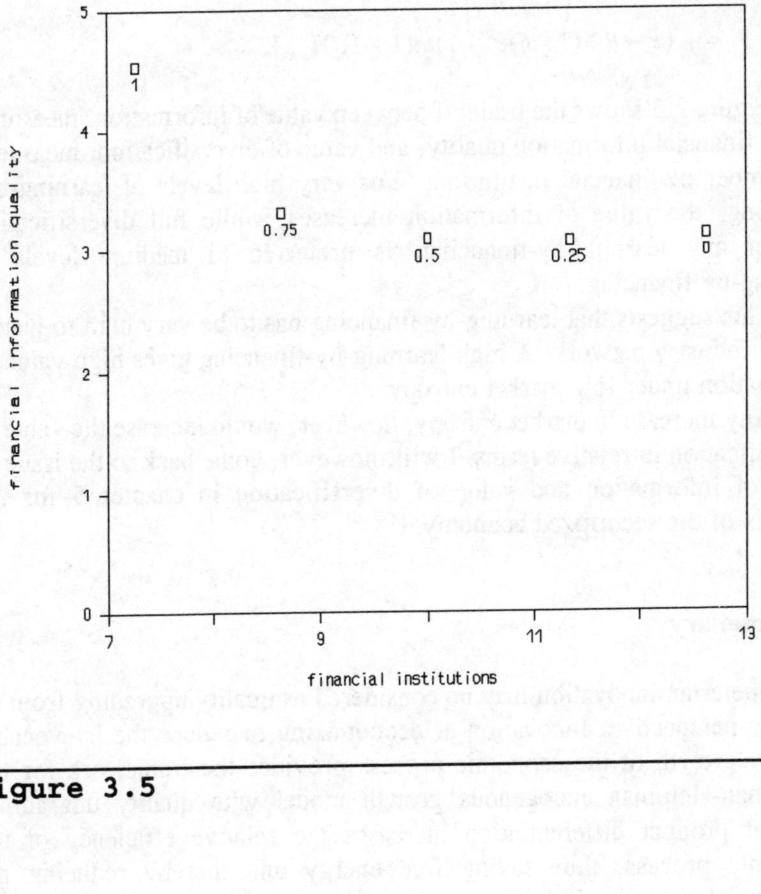
financial information quality
financial institutions
5
4
3
2
1
0
7
9
11
13
1
0.75
0.5
0.25
0

Figure 3.5

$$(3.26)\quad C = \frac{e^{\lambda}}{\theta+(1-\theta)e^{\lambda}} + log_2(\theta+(1-\theta)e^{\lambda}),$$

and the number of financial institutions:

$$(3.27)\quad P = -(e^{\lambda}+\theta+(1-\theta)e^{\lambda}-1)ln(1-H/H_{max}).$$

Figure 3.5 shows the tradeoff between value of information, measured by the financial information quality, and value of diversification, measured by number of financial institutions. For very high levels of learning-by-financing, the value of information increases, while full diversification without any learning-by-financing, is preferred to medium levels of learning-by-financing.

This suggests that learning-by-financing has to be very high to justify a bank-industry network. A high learning-by-financing gives high value of information under low market entropy.

Any increase in market entropy, however, would increase the value of diversification in relative terms. I will, however, come back to the issue of value of information and value of diversification in chapter 5 for the analysis of the securitized economy.

3.8 Summary

Schumpeterian innovation may be considered as quality upgrading from an entropy perspective. Innovation as economizing to reduce the irrevocable entropy growth of the economic process provides the framework for the Grossman-Helpman endogenous growth model with quality upgrading. Vertical product differentiation increases the relative efficiency of the economic process, thus saving free energy and thereby reducing the increase of entropy. This requires the existence of a set of conventions which gives a social selection mechanism for quality ladder viability. Only the quality ladders with sufficiently low negative externalities remain viable. This chapter extended the Grossman-Helpman model to include banks and asymmetric information between bankers.

The extended model has been used to compare various growth regimes with respect to their learning-by-financing. Three simulation rounds show that learning-by-financing increases innovativeness. The first one with sixteen growth regimes shows that learning-by-financing increases innovativeness, because learning-by-financing within bank-industry networks gives a better resource allocation and provides the less informed market investors a reliable signal concerning entrepreneurial qualities of firms.

The more distant the cooperation between banks and industry, the noisier this signal becomes, creating an interest rate spread which increases the costs of knowledge capital. A combination of a high learning-by-financing, a low riskfree interest rate, a high R&D productivity, decreasing entry costs, and large quality increments, yielding substantial entrepreneurial rents, gives the highest innovativeness. Since low entry costs in combination with high entrepreneurial rents give, *ceteris paribus*, the highest innovativeness, I made two additional rounds to study how the financial system determines this combination.

In the second simulation round with eight regimes, I used different financial system equilibria, based on learning-by-financing to endogenize the quality increments to be a function of learning-by-financing and the riskfree interest rate. The higher the learning-by-financing, given the riskfree interest rate, the larger the quality increments are, because of lower costs of knowledge capital.

In the third simulation round with four growth regimes, the R&D productivity at perfect resource allocation is made dependent on learning-by-financing. The higher the learning-by-financing, given the riskfree interest rate, the lower the entry costs are, because the R&D productivity increases. In other words, the R&D productivity at perfect resource allocation is an outcome of the R&D factor allocation that learning-by-financing permits through the positive voice mechanism of bank-industry networks.

Hence, the better the learning-by-financing, the higher technological risks may be taken without increasing financial fragility. This is the reason why higher learning-by-financing yields a higher leverage effect, the product of debt/equity ratio and Wicksellian capital market disequilibrium.

Industrial market entropy, i.e. market uncertainty, decreases with learning-by-financing, while financial information quality improves only at very high levels of learning-by-financing. There is a tradeoff between value of information, financial information quality, and the value of diversification, the number of financial institutions. The value of information is higher when the market entropy is lower, while the value of diversification increases with higher market entropy. Yet, a high value of information requires a very high learning-by-financing.

Main Symbols

ι: aggregate innovative intensity (innovativeness)
θ: learning-by-financing
ρ: riskfree interest rate
L: total labor supply
a: ratio of R&D labor to innovativeness at perfect resource allocation
L/a: R&D productivity of the economy at perfect resource allocation (ratio of innovativeness to the share of total labor supply employed in R&D)
λ: quality increment
δ: inverse quality increment (labor costs)
φ: ratio of debt costs to labor costs
v: firm value at perfect resource allocation
v_m: stock market value of the firm
V: inverse stock market value
ε: entrepreneurial rent
p_Q: quality adjusted price
H: market entropy
n: number of potential leaders
C: financial information quality
P: number of financial institutions as information processors

Notes

1. See Segerstrom, Anant, and Dinopoulos (1990) for a Schumpeterian product life cycle model and Aghion and Howitt (1992) for a Schumpeterian creative destruction model. Grossman and Helpman (1991a,b) have combined these two models into a single quality ladder model.

2. A firm is an institution defined, not as a legal unit, but as a set of knowledge characteristics at each period of time. Hence, since a real world firm evolves continuously over time, the firm is an historical institution which constitute two different firms at two different periods of its history.

3. Grossman and Helpman (1991a) do not distinguish debt from equity. The two level financing hierarchy, which I use, allow for considering private equity identical

with private debt, on the one hand, and public equity with public debt, on the other hand.

4. In the credit-based financial systems, close bank-industry links make it possible for banks to analyze the prospects of future profitability without having to rely as much as market-based systems on past performance and collateral. Obviously, this system difference is due to differences in information production (and confidence building) between the systems.

5. This is the increase in the interest rate spread with respect to stock market value due to the variation in the probability of the noisy signal being true. Gertler, Hubbard and Kashyap (1991) define the spread as the difference between the firm's marginal cost of finance and the riskless rate, in this context given by:

$S = (1/\text{prob}(\tilde{\gamma}=\tilde{v}|v) - 1)\rho$.

6. This is essentially the same idea as Diamond's (1984) delegated monitoring performed by financial intermediaries. Monitoring costs are reduced when the depositors may delegate to an intermediary the task of monitoring instead of doing it themselves, each one of them causing duplication. Information production works in the same way. There are costs involved in establishing an ongoing history of interaction to informationally capture a firm. The costs are lower when this task is delegated to banks. This is the economic rationale for bank-industry networks, a rationale which holds also in a securitized economy.

7. See chapter 2 for an analysis of this problem, brought up by Minsky (1990), where I make a case for the strong bank-industry networks contributing to a relatively higher compatibility of financial and industrial innovation.

8. Note here that labor productivity in R&D at perfect resource allocation, the maximum ratio of innovativeness to R&D labor employed, is denoted by 1/a. Expressing R&D labor as a share of total labor supply, which is kept fixed, gives L/a.

9. Keeping L fixed, L/a is only able to increase through a higher R&D productivity, 1/a, thus, decreasing the entry costs, wa, and exit costs, v, since $v=wa$ if $\iota>0$. The aggregate innovative competence is hereby improved. The higher the δ, the lower the quality increments, λ, are, thus decreasing the innovative difficulty, since the required quality improvement step for an innovation is lower. Consequently, the entrepreneurial rents, $\epsilon=1 - \delta(1+\varphi)$, are smaller. An increase in R&D productivity, the innovative competence, would in this case be a waste of knowledge capital.

10. Note that there is to Schumpeterian entrepreneurs a δ_{max} above which they would not innovate because the value of the transient monopoly is too limited.

11. This is a simplifying assumption which may be considerably more complex in an evolutionary context. The evolution of such a decision rule and its viability are very involved, but history produces information about the actual yield of the additional purchasing power.

12. The Wicksellian capital market disequilibrium arises whenever the natural rate of interest - operational profit to assets - exceeds the market rate of interest - the corporate interest rate (Wicksell 1898, 1906). Eliasson's (1985) proof that a Wicksellian capital market disequilibrium is necessary for maintaining innovation has to be reformulated, because he defines entrepreneurial rent as the Wicksellian capital market disequilibrium, while I define entrepreneurial rent as the return on entrepreneurship.

Using equation (3.21), the capital market is in equilibrium, $(1 - \delta)/A_m = \rho+S$, whenever the entrepreneurial rent to equity is equal to the managerial return to equity, $\epsilon V^* = \rho+S$. Substituting this into equation (3.10) and arranging terms, give a dynamic equilibrium with $\iota^*=0$. Of course, in our entropy context, we are only interested in qualitative growth, so we require $\iota^*>0$, but this is possible only when the entrepreneurial rents to equity are larger than managerial returns to equity, $\epsilon V^* > \rho+S$, which in turn requires a Wicksellian capital market disequilibrium, $(1 - \delta)/A_m > \rho+S$.

13. Yakushiji defines market entropy at time t as $H_t = -\Sigma_i s_t^i \log s_t^i$ where s_t^i is the market share of firm i at time t.

14. The regimes are $\theta = \{0.0; 0.25; 0.5; 0.75; 1.0\}$. For all regimes, $\rho = 0.02$, $y = 20$, and $z = 6$. The model is the same as in the case with four growth regimes.

15. Radner's formula for the delay is $C=(N/Q)+\log_2(Q)$ and for the number of processors $P=(N+Q - 1)/T$ where N is the number of items, Q the number of information processors assigned to a cohort of information, and T the arrival time for a cohort of information. I let N increase with the quality increments and Q decrease from N to 1 as the learning-by-financing goes from 0 to 1. The arrival time for new information decreases with higher market entropy.

4 Schumpeterian Banker-Entrepreneur Interaction and the Evolution of Bank-Industry Networks: Spontaneous Order or Collective Action?[1]

4.1 The Institutional Learning-by-Financing Process

Learning-by-financing is the function upon which the bank-industry networks are founded, but what propagation mechanisms make them evolve? Does the history of social interaction between bankers and entrepreneurs yield a spontaneous evolution of bank-industry networks or is collective action required for its institutionalization? What guides the institutional dynamics of banker-entrepreneur interaction?

This corresponds to the two conjectures for analysis of the propagation process of economic institutions, identified by Witt (1989); the Smith-Menger-Hayek conjecture of spontaneous order, on the one hand, and the Olson-Buchanan-Tullock conjecture of collective action, on the other hand.

New institutional economics[2] follows the spontaneous order conjecture by focusing on function rather than intention, but requires sufficient institutional endowments to sustain the function. Insufficient institutional endowments require collective action - the design of privileged groups (Olson, 1965, Sandler, 1992) - to start the spontaneous evolution. Learning-by-financing, the function explaining bank-industry networks, requires institutional endowments, such as developed banking and a preference for network commitment.

Consider the bank-industry network as a convention of organizing economic competence and let institutional endowments determine the combination of propagation mechanisms. Following Pelikan (1989), the bank-industry network can be seen as a structure of economic competence whose evolution depends on the prevailing regime, defined as the combination of propagation mechanisms. Large institutional endowments allow the regime to be spontaneous order-oriented, while small institutional endowments require a more collective action-oriented regime.

In this chapter, I will analyze Schumpeterian banker-entrepreneur interaction as an evolutionary Stag Hunt game; evolutionary, because the banker and the entrepreneur interact strategically as satisficing agents in a world with uncertainty and bounded rationality, and Stag Hunt, because they would be better off by cooperating within a bank-industry network, but only if both of them do so. As the network benefits require mutual cooperation, there is no reward for defection when the other cooperates, thus ruling out the Prisoners' Dilemma game. In fact, all games which reward defection when the other cooperates are ruled out from the analysis.

Banker-entrepreneur interaction within a bank-industry network involves coordination rather than opportunistic behavior. The Stag Hunt game is an intermediary game between the Prisoners' Dilemma and the Coordination game (Ullmann-Margalit, 1977). Hence, the spontaneous evolution of bank-industry networks may be analyzed as an evolutionary Stag Hunt game. The two evolutionary stable strategies of this game are, in the sense of Sugden's (1986) definition, the spontaneously evolved conventions of industrial innovation finance: (i) the bank convention with bankers and entrepreneurs cooperating within bank-industry networks and (ii) the bond convention with independent bankers and entrepreneurs.

My purpose is to show how bank-industry networks, based on mutual trust and network commitment, evolve spontaneously due to learning-by-financing only when the institutional endowments - network commitment and developed banking - are sufficient, and that some collective action might be necessary to make the spontaneous evolution of bank-industry networks feasible. The Stag Hunt model will be applied to Sweden as a case of a spontaneous evolution of bank-industry networks and France as a case where collective action was required.

A functionalist-evolutionary[3] explanation why bank-industry networks exist, requires that Elster's (1979) five criteria are fulfilled. The bank-industry network is an institution explained by its function learning-by-financing for bankers and entrepreneurs if and only if:

(i) learning-by-financing is an effect of the bank-industry network;

(ii) learning-by-financing is beneficial for bankers and entrepreneurs;

(iii) learning-by-financing is unintended by the actors producing the bank-industry network;

(iv) learning-by-financing is unrecognized by the banker and the entrepreneur;

(v) learning-by-financing maintains the bank-industry network by a causal feedback loop passing through the decision-making of bankers and entrepreneurs.

With banker-entrepreneur interaction as an evolutionary Stag Hunt game, the population of bankers and the population of entrepreneurs interact strategically, each individual player following a strategy which is a fixed satisficing rule due to uncertainty and bounded rationality. There are no attempts to form a club in order to design a network. Learning-by-financing is a function, not an intention. The bankers and the entrepreneurs choose their respective strategy and the viability of each strategy depends on its relative fitness in the own population, given the strategy mix of the other population. The criteria above are, thus, fulfilled and the network evolves by strategic interaction between satisficing agents in the Stag Hunt game, not by design.

My approach will be that of spontaneous order, along the lines of Sugden (1986), comparing the bank convention, based on bank-industry networks, and the bond convention which does not have any such networks. In this respect, it is an invisible hand explanation according to the Popper-Hayek program (Langlois, 1986). This explanation represents spontaneous order, but the collective preferences are subject to collective action through selective incentives or the design of institutional structures (Olson, 1965). In this context, I will analyze the evolution of bank-industry networks as the design of privileged groups (Olson, 1965, Sandler, 1992). The collective action evolution of bank-industry networks may be analyzed as an evolutionary Fully Privileged Stag Hunt game.

Section 4.2 analyzes the bank-industry network as a spontaneous order in an evolutionary Stag Hunt game. Section 4.3 considers the evolution of bank-industry networks by collective action. Section 4.4 compares the spontaneous evolution of bank-industry networks in Sweden and France, while section 4.5 considers the role of collective action in these two countries. Section 4.6 gives a summary.

4.2 The Bank-Industry Network as a Spontaneous Order in an Evolutionary Stag Hunt Game

Considering institutions as spontaneously emerged order in a world with bounded rationality, implies that an institution is a convention having evolved through a process of social interaction. A convention is, thus, an evolutionary stable strategy, ESS, in an evolutionary game with two or more possible ESSs (Sugden, 1986).[4] Modelling banker-entrepreneur interaction and its institutionalization would, therefore, require an evolutionary game with at least two ESSs.

A game fulfilling this requirement is the Stag Hunt game. Basically, it tells that hunters may individually catch rabbits, but they would all be better off if all of them would cooperate in order to hunt a stag.

There are two evolutionary stable strategies, ESSs,[5] each one corresponding to a convention; individual rabbit hunting and collective stag hunting, the latter being the preferred convention which requires cooperation.

How does this game relate to banker-entrepreneur interaction? Essentially the collective stag hunt represents banker-entrepreneur interaction within a bank-industry network and individual rabbit hunting arm's length interaction between bankers and entrepreneurs, giving the maximum security level, but not the big entrepreneurial rents.

The two evolutionary stable strategies of this game are, in the sense of Sugden's (1986) definition, the spontaneously evolved conventions of industrial innovation finance:

(i) The bank convention institutionalizes banker-entrepreneur interaction within bank-industry networks, establishing a durable link between bankers and entrepreneurs. Learning-by-financing is possible, so the banker may use private information. Hence, the bank convention implies private information for all financial instruments.

(ii) The bond convention institutionalizes banker-entrepreneur interaction as a market contract, establishing a temporary link. There is no learning-by-financing, so the banker has to rely on public information available at the market, performing a monitoring function. Hence, the bond convention implies public information for all financial instruments.

Along each quality ladder of the economy, bankers and entrepreneurs play for each innovation a two-person random pairing game between a member of the population of bankers and a member of the population of entrepreneurs. As there is behavioral uncertainty, bankers and entrepreneurs may meet again without remembering the behavioral strategy of the other player. The banker may learn about the innovative skills of the entrepreneur through learning-by-financing, but not about the reliability of the entrepreneur. A reliable entrepreneur today might be an unreliable entrepreneur tomorrow.

There are two strategies; strategy 1 being network-oriented and strategy 2 being independent-minded. The banker chooses between either strategy 1 (informed) of being a network bank or strategy 2 (arm's length) of being an independent bank, behaving like a market investor in the latter case. Similarly, the entrepreneur chooses between either strategy 1 (reliable) of staying within the network and strategy 2 (unreliable) of taking the credit as a temporary link with the banker.

Consider the ex post payoffs for successful innovations in order to focus on the differences in information costs. Like Pelikan (1989), I consider the optimal structure as an outcome of exceptional successes of the evolutionary process. The spontaneous order propagation is efficient as long as it provides conventions which minimize the interaction costs of Schumpeterian failures.

The payoffs will, therefore, measure the net benefits of the two conventions. Set the payoff of independent bankers and entrepreneurs to unity and let, as a consequence of private information, $\alpha > 1$ denote the payoff of the network banker and $\omega > 1$ the payoff of the network entrepreneur. This gives the payoff structure of the Stag Hunt game illustrated in Table 4.1.

Assume that the shares of network bankers and network entrepreneurs are random at the initial stage of each game. For each vintage of innovations, i.e. an innovation cluster based on the same vintage of knowledge capital, the networks are reborn. The growth regime remains viable as long as it creates new vintages of innovations, which requires institutional support from the financial system.

Lock-in (David, 1985, Arthur, 1988) may occur randomly, so learning-by-financing built up around the old vintage of innovations may be relevant or irrelevant for the new one in a random fashion, thus making the initial distribution of strategies random for each vintage of innovations. Hence, the institutional dynamics of the game give the probabilities of convergence to the bank convention and bond convention, respectively.

Furthermore, assume that the life time of a vintage of innovations is shorter than the time required to reach either of the two conventions, which would be the end of history. In other words, vintages of innovations arrive frequently, thus shaking up the process of institutional change. Hence, the institutional dynamics make the financial system an evolving combination of the bank convention and the bond convention.

Table 4.1 Banker-Entrepreneur Interaction as a Stag Hunt Game

		Entrepreneur	
		1 Reliable	2 Unreliable
Banker	1 Informed	α,ω	0,1
	2 Arm's length	1,0	1,1

Let p denote the proportion of bankers using strategy 1 (informed) in the population of bankers and q the proportion of entrepreneurs using strategy 1 (reliable) in the population of entrepreneurs. Then the population dynamics of the pair (p,q) represent the institutional dynamics of banker-entrepreneur interaction guiding the evolution of bank-industry networks.

The payoff matrix of Table 4.1 and the shares of network-oriented bankers and entrepreneurs, p and q respectively, lead to a system of two differential equations describing the population dynamics of bankers and entrepreneurs. Let us assume Malthusian dynamics, so the growth rate of a strategy is equal to its relative fitness. Hence, a strategy grows as long as its fitness is higher than the average fitness of the population (Friedman, 1991). Therefore, the growth of informed bankers becomes:

(4.1) $\dot{p} = p(\alpha q-1)(1-p)$,

and the growth of reliable entrepreneurs:

(4.2) $\dot{q} = q(\omega p-1)(1-q)$.

Equation (4.1) shows that the proportion of informed bankers in the population of bankers is stable when $p = 0;1$ or $q = 1/\alpha$. Similarly, equation (4.2) shows that the proportion of reliable entrepreneurs in the population of entrepreneurs is stable when $q = 0;1$ or $p = 1/\omega$.

As shown by Friedman (1991), the ESSs of a game whose population dynamics are given by a system of differential equations are stable equilibria identified through a local stability analysis of the Jacobian created by this system.

Let us, therefore, carry out a local stability analysis of the system consisting of equations (4.1) and (4.2), studying the determinant and the trace of the Jacobian. The determinant of the Jacobian of the system of equations (4.1) and (4.2) is:

(4.3) $\det J = (\alpha q-1)(1-2p)(\omega p-1)(1-2q)-\alpha\omega pq(1-p)(1-q)$,

while the trace of the Jacobian is:

(4.4) $\text{tr } J = (\alpha q-1)(1-2p)+(\omega p-1)(1-2q)$.

The results of the local stability analysis of the five equilibrium points are summarized in Table 4.2.

Table 4.2 Results of the local stability analysis

Equilibrium	det J	tr J	Result
$p=0,q=0$	$1>0$	$-2<0$	ESS
$p=0,q=1$	$\alpha-1>0$	$\alpha>0$	unstable
$p=1,q=0$	$\omega-1>0$	$\omega>0$	unstable
$p=1,q=1$	$(\alpha-1)(\omega-1)>0$	$2-\alpha-\omega<0$	ESS
$p=1/\omega,q=1/\alpha$	$-(1-1/\omega)(1-1/\alpha)<0$	0	saddle point

Hence, dynamic analysis (local stability analysis) gives the two ESSs of the Stag Hunt game: ($p=0,q=0$) and ($p=1,q=1$), each one corresponding to a convention: (i) the bond convention with independent banks and firms ($p=0,q=0$) and (ii) the bank convention with bank-industry networks ($p=1,q=1$). There are, in addition, two unstable equilibria, ($p=0,q=1$) and ($p=1,q=0$), as well as a saddle point, ($p=1/\omega,q=1/\alpha$).

The institutional dynamics of banker-entrepreneur interaction converge for all points to the right of the line ($p=0,q=1$)($p=1/\omega,q=1/\alpha$)($p=1,q=0$) to the bank convention and for all points to the left of this line to the bond convention.

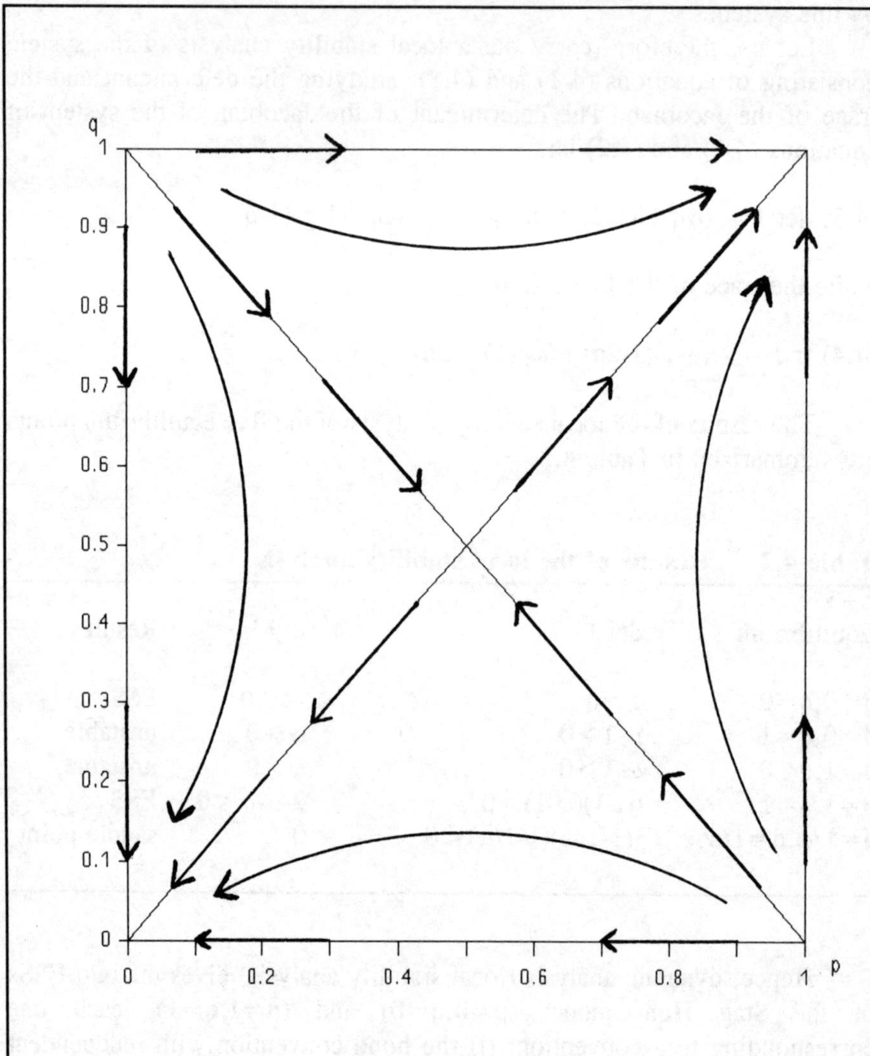

Figure 4.1

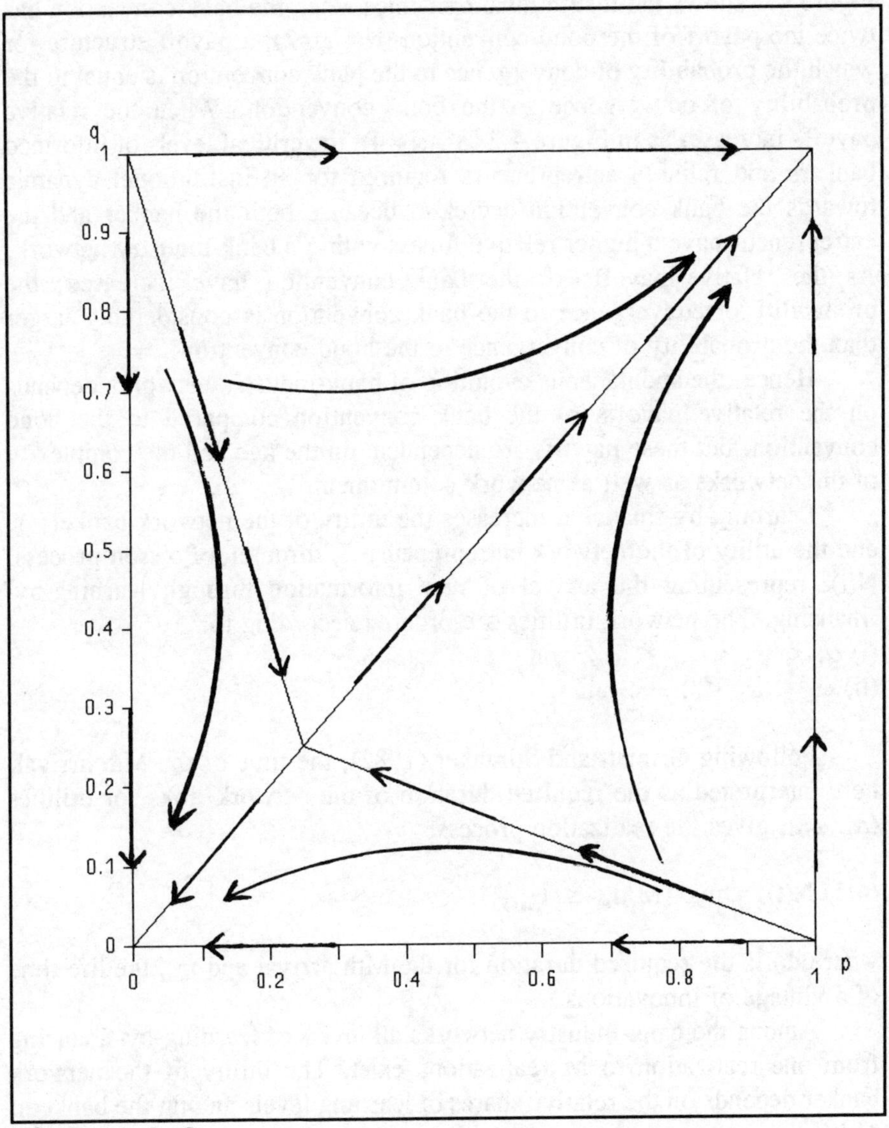

Figure 4.2

Figure 4.1 shows the institutional dynamics when the bank convention has twice the payoff of the bond convention ($\alpha=\omega=2$), a payoff structure for which the probability of convergence to the bank convention is equal to the probability of convergence to the bond convention. When the relative payoffs increase, as in Figure 4.2 ($\alpha=\omega=4$), the critical levels of informed bankers and reliable entrepreneurs required for an institutional dynamic towards the bank convention decrease, because both the banker and the entrepreneur have a higher relative fitness within a bank-industry network. As the relative payoffs of the bank convention have increased, the probability of convergence to the bank convention is considerably larger than the probability of convergence to the bond convention.

Hence, the spontaneous evolution of bank-industry networks depends on the relative payoffs of the bank convention compared to the bond convention, but these payoffs are dependent on the age and the complexity of the networks as well as network commitment.

Learning-by-financing increases the utility of the network banker, α, and the utility of the network entrepreneur, ω, through a Poisson process, N(t), representing the arrival of new information through learning-by-financing. The network utilities are ordered according to:

(i) $\alpha_1 < \alpha_2 < ... < \alpha_M$, and

(ii) $\omega_1 < \omega_2 < ... < \omega_M$.

Following Grimett and Stirzaker (1982), the time of the Mth arrival, here interpreted as the required duration of the network links for utilities (α_M,ω_M), gives the realization process:

$$(4.5)\ N(t) = \max\{M{:}d_M \leq t_{max}\},$$

where d_M is the required duration for the Mth arrival and t_{max} the life time of a vintage of innovations.

Among the bank-industry networks all levels of learning-by-financing from one realization to M realizations exist. The utility of the network banker depends on the relative shares of learning levels among the bankers:

$$(4.6)\ \alpha = \sum_{i=1}^{M} s_i\alpha_i,$$

where α_i is the utility of the network bankers who have achieved the ith level of learning-by-financing and s_i their share among network bankers.

Similarly, the utility of the network entrepreneurs depends on the relative shares of learning-by-financing levels:

$$(4.7)\ \omega = \sum_{i=1}^{M} s_i\omega_i,$$

where ω_i is the utility of the network entrepreneurs whose bankers have achieved the ith level of learning-by-financing and s_i their share among network entrepreneurs.

Equations (4.5), (4.6), and (4.7) imply that the higher the share of networks with long duration, giving a high level of learning-by-financing, the higher the network utilities of bankers and entrepreneurs become. Hence, a long average network duration gives a high probability of convergence to the bank convention. In other words, the higher the share of old, viable networks, the stronger the bank convention is in the economy. As networks have to be reborn for each vintage of innovations, a high age means a high durability.

For simplicity, assume that the shares of all the utility levels are equal. If learning-by-financing becomes more difficult for a new vintage of innovations, while competence remains unchanged due to lock-in, thus increasing the required durations, then the arrival of new information through learning-by-financing decreases due to a lower M, according to equation (4.5). As M decreases, the network utilities decrease as well, according to equations (4.6) and (4.7). Hence, lock-in decreases the relative fitness of the bank convention, but entry, reorganization, rationalization, and exit, along the lines of Eliasson (1996), create new competence which will keep bank-industry networks viable.

A long network duration within a traditional bank-industry network gives a high learning-by-financing, i.e. a rapid arrival of private information, for innovation strategies based on intangible, firm- and network-specific assets, but may not do so for innovation strategies based on emerging technologies. This kind of lock-in into previously successful choices has been studied by Glete (1998) and Ballot and Taymaz (1998).

In the case of an emerging technology, a bank-industry network around a venture capitalist with short network durations may give a higher learning-by-financing, because negative network externalities are weaker. Negative network externalities create a critical mass of adopters rather than lock-in (Witt, 1997). Hence, the traditional bank-industry network may still be able to adapt to an emerging technology, although it requires a higher critical mass of adopters. In the model, M will remain low for emerging technologies, until the critical mass has been reached, and is restored thereafter.

The network utilities are positive functions of learning-by-financing, θ, i.e. $\alpha'(\theta) > 0$ and $\omega'(\theta) > 0$. Consider a network between a banker and entrepreneurs A, B, and C, where there are links between the banker and each entrepreneur as well as between the entrepreneurs. As an abstract representation of real world bank-industry groups, this kind of network gives learning-by-financing both directly through the links between the banker and each entrepreneur and indirectly through the links between the entrepreneurs.

For entrepreneur A, there exists a trade-off between the duration of the link between the banker and entrepreneur A, on the one hand, and the average duration of the links between the banker and entrepreneurs B and C, respectively:

$$(4.8)\ d^A(d^B+d^C)/2 = c,$$

where d^A, d^B, and d^C are the durations of the link between the banker and entrepreneurs A, B, and C, respectively, and c network commitment between entrepreneurs. The higher the network commitment between entrepreneurs, c, the longer duration d^A is possible without decreasing the durations d^B and d^C.

Network complexity implies that learning-by-financing about entrepreneur A is a joint product between the duration of the link between the banker and entrepreneur A and the sum of the duration of all links between the banker and the entrepreneur within the network:

$$(4.9)\ \theta_A = l_{pri}d^A + l_{pub}(d^A + d^B + d^C).$$

A more complex network implies that the sum of all the links between the banker and the entrepreneurs belonging to the network is more important compared to the direct link between the banker and the entrepreneur. The more complex the network, the larger l_{pub} is relative to

l_{pri}. Hence, the higher the network complexity, the more learning-by-financing about entrepreneur A benefits from learning across all links between the banker and the set of entrepreneurs belonging to the network.

As the sum of all the links matter to network complexity, the latter is dependent on network commitment between entrepreneurs. Equations (4.8) and (4.9) give the network commitment dependent learning-by-financing function:

$$(4.10)\ \theta_A = l_{pri}d^A + l_{pub}(d^A + 2c/d^A).$$

The higher the network commitment between entrepreneurs, c, the higher the contribution network complexity may yield to learning-by-financing about entrepreneur A.

Consider negative network externalities again, starting with the case of an increase in learning-by-financing difficulty for a new vintage of innovations, while competence remains unchanged due to lock-in. In equation (4.10) both l_{pri} and l_{pub} decrease, thus decreasing the effect network duration has on learning-by-financing. The required duration to achieve the same level of learning-by-financing increases. Provided the life time of an innovation, t_{max}, remains unchanged, equation (4.5) implies that the number of arrivals of new information has to decrease, i.e. **M** becomes lower. Hence, the network utilities decrease, according to equations (4.6) and (4.7).

Again, the relative fitness of the bank convention decreases, unless entry, reorganization, rationalization, and exit keep bank-industry networks viable. When negative network externalities create a critical mass of adopters for emerging technologies rather than lock-in, l_{pri} and l_{pub} remain low until the critical mass has been reached, and are restored thereafter.

Summing up, the older and more viable the networks and the higher their complexity and network commitment, the higher the network utilities become, thus making the bank convention stronger in the economy.

4.3 Collective Action and the Evolution of Bank-Industry Networks

In the previous section, various levels of network utilities have been compared. In this section, the actual value is going to be determined in order to analyze when collective action is necessary. Using a collective action approach (Olson, 1965, Sandler, 1992), the relative payoffs of network bankers and entrepreneurs in the Stag Hunt game may be endogenized. Collective action problems are not limited to Prisoners' Dilemma games and any game structure is applicable to more than one configuration of costs, technology of public supply, and tastes (Sandler, 1992). Hence, the bank-industry network has to be regarded as a privileged group where the network-specific information, the private information obtained by network banks, is a public good for network members only. The network produces joint products, giving a private utility, entrepreneurial rents and interest payments divided within the network, as well as a public utility, the institutional endowments. In other words, there is an endowment effect which implies that initial property rights are not neutral, thus contradicting the Coase theorem (Kahneman, Knetch, and Thaler, 1990).[6]

A developed banking system and a historically evolved preference for network commitment between banker and entrepreneurs are crucial institutional endowments. A developed banking system is, of course, essential for the willingness of the entrepreneur to turn to the banker, but the commitment between banker and entrepreneur after an initial successful cooperation determines the possibilities for learning-by-financing.

Network commitment may be seen as a Becker (1992) habit, but if agents have pragmatic rationality, then network commitment represents a resolute behavior, in the sense of Sugden (1991), a Kantian self-imposed law or a Humean desire to stick to past behavior of commitment. Moral sentiment induces commitment (Frank, 1988), but moral sentiment is in itself a historically evolved convention, an underlying satisficing rule.

Suppose that each unit of network-specific information, for an entrepreneur, yields one unit of private utility and k units of public utility. Let E_i denote the ratio of bank convention entrepreneurial rents to bond convention entrepreneurial rents and R_i the ratio of bank convention interest payments to bond convention interest payments. E_i and R_i, thus, indicate the ratio of value of information to value of diversification. A network banker holds equity shares of the entrepreneur's firm, because there is a minimum equity share that a bank has to hold in the firm to maintain a stable customer relationship between bank and firm as well as a legal maximum share (Aoki, 1988). Assume that the banker holds the minimum share needed to maintain the network learning-by-financing, σ, and market investors the rest. Hence, the network banker's private utility depends, in addition to interest payments, R_i, on the entrepreneur's utility according to the banker's share of corporate equity, $\sigma\omega_i$.

If network utility is a joint product between one unit of private utility and k units of public utility determined by summation of the private utilities, then the utility of the network banker becomes:

$$(4.11)\ \alpha_i = R_i + \sigma\omega_i + k(E_i + R_i),\ i = 1,2,\ldots,M,$$

where the utility of the network entrepreneur is:

$$(4.12)\ \omega_i = E_i + k(E_i + R_i),\ i = 1,2,\ldots,M.$$

A developed industrial banking system with strong bank-industry networks and efficient learning-by-financing implies that E_i and R_i are high, something which increases the relative payoffs of the bank convention. These payoffs depend, however, not only on the return of the banker and the entrepreneur, but also on the institutional endowments' increasing the public utility within the network through a higher k. Provided banking is developed, k represents the institutional endowment effect of network commitment.

A weak network commitment between banker and entrepreneur, reflected in a non-positive k, would give low network utilities which rely on the individual pecuniary payoff, as the public utility of the institutional endowments is non-positive. In this case, a spontaneous evolution of bank-industry networks may not be feasible, since the utility for each network duration is lower. The probability of convergence to the bank convention decreases. Collective action, designing the bank-industry network as a fully privileged group, may solve this problem. The rules of the game change, as collective action transforms the payoff structure of the Stag Hunt game into the Fully Privileged Stag Hunt Game of Table 4.3.

Table 4.3 Banker-Entrepreneur Interaction as a Fully Privileged Stag Hunt Game

		Entrepreneur	
		1 Reliable	2 Unreliable
Banker	1 Informed	2,2	0,1
	2 Arm's length	1,0	-1,-1

This payoff structure gives another dynamic system of the evolution of network-oriented bankers and entrepreneurs:

(4.13) $\dot{p} = p(1-p)$,

(4.14) $\dot{q} = q(1-q)$.

The system given by equations (4.13) and (4.14) have, as shown in Table 4.4, four equilibria, but only one ESS: (p=1,q=1), that is the bank convention, while the bond convention (p=0,q=0) is an unstable equilibrium, (p=1,q=0) and (p=0,q=1) being saddle points. Hence, the bank convention is the dominant strategy, since networks are fully privileged, thus giving the dynamics of Figure 4.3.

Table 4.4 Results of the local stability analysis

Equilibrium	det J	tr J	Result
p=0,q=0	1>0	2>0	unstable
p=0,q=1	-1<0	0	saddle point
p=1,q=0	-1<0	0	saddle point
p=1,q=1	1>0	-2<0	ESS

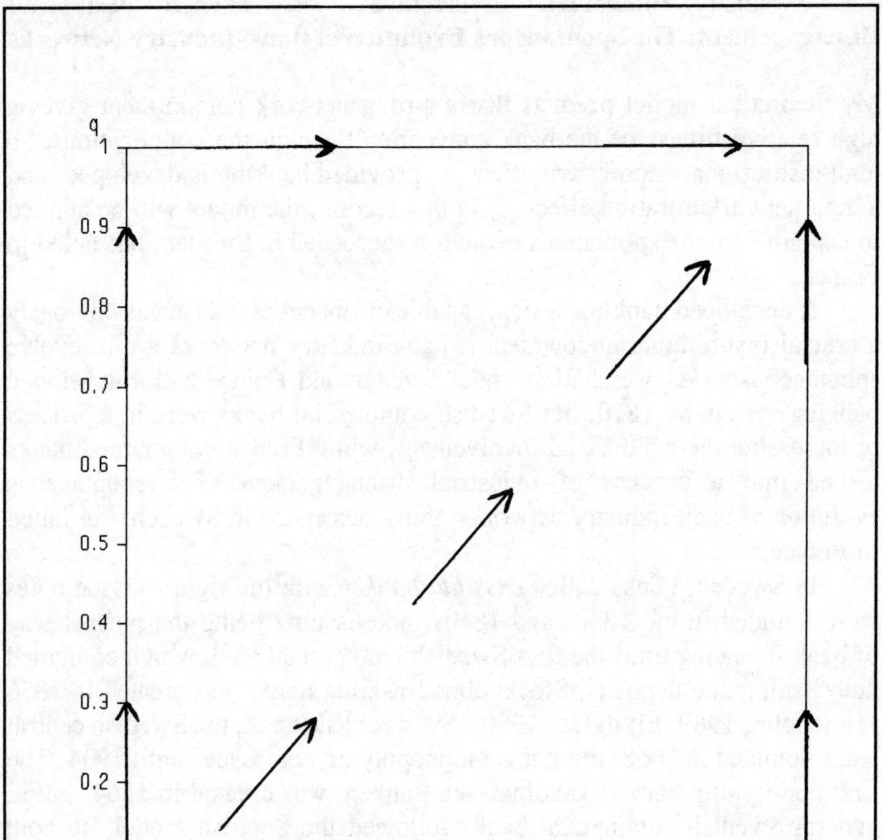

Figure 4.3

4.4 Swedish Industrial Involvement vs. French Industrial Disengagement: The Spontaneous Evolution of Bank-Industry Networks

My theoretical model predicts that a strong network commitment gives a high relative fitness of the bank convention through the combination of a high institutional endowment effect, k, provided banking is developed, and a high network duration effect, c. In this section, the model will be applied to explain why the spontanous evolution succeeded in Sweden, but failed in France.

A developed banking system capable of financing industry is obviously a crucial institutional endowment if bank-industry networks are to evolve spontaneously. As we shall se, both Sweden and France had a developed banking system by 1870, but Swedish commercial banks were in a process of increasing their industrial involvement, while French commercial banks turned into a process of industrial disengagement. The spontaneous evolution of bank-industry networks, thus, succeeded in Sweden, but failed in France.

In Sweden, banks called *enskilda banker* with the right to issue notes were founded in the 1830s and 1840s, note-issuing being the normal way of bank financing until the first Swedish commercial bank which combined note-issuing and deposits, Stockholms Enskilda Bank, was created in 1856 (Thunholm, 1989, Lindgren, 1990). Sveriges Riksbank, the Swedish central bank, founded in 1668, did not get monopoly on note issues until 1904. The first non-issuing bank, Skandinaviska Banken, was created in 1864, but in general Swedish commercial banks followed the Scottish model, so both note issues and deposits were used as basis for bank lending (Larsson and Lindgren, 1992).

Commercial banks got a new business opportunity as the merchant/trading houses were unable to provide sufficient venture capital during Sweden's industrialization, taking off in the 1890s. Swedish banks established long-term involvement in industry with underwriting of industrial bonds and shares as well as structural reorganizations, along the lines of German universal banking (Lindgren, 1990, and Larsson and Lindgren, 1992).

In France, the central bank, Banque de France, founded in 1800, got a monopoly on note issues in 1848. John Law had introduced note-issuing banking with the creation of Banque Générale in 1716, but overissue and speculation in shares led to the Mississippi Bubble in 1720 (Davies, 1994).

The Banque de France sustained the local bankers, in themselves more geared towards commerce than industry, thus expanding credit (Plessis, 1987).

Commercial banking improved during the third quarter of the 19th century with the creation of Crédit Industriel et Commercial in 1859, Crédit Lyonnais in 1863, Société Générale pour Favoriser le Dévéloppment du Commerce et de l'Industrie en France in 1864, and Paribas in 1872, so that industry had access to continuous short-term credit (Davies, 1994). The big banks were also active in underwriting of industrial bonds and shares, while the industrial regions in the North (Nord and Pas de Calais) and East (Meurthe et Moselle) had their own regional banks geared to industry (Freedeman, 1993, and Gueslin, 1992).

The prototype for industrial banking was Crédit Mobilier which had been set up in 1852, but its failure in 1867 made the risks of long-term industrial involvement apparent. Crédit Mobilier had been a universal bank, the first French deposit bank, but the 1870-1945 period became one of gradual industrial disengagement and separation between commercial banks and *banques d'affaires* (Bellon, 1980). This functional separation between commercial banks and *banques d'affaires* was induced by bank failures and was legally confirmed after World War II (Davies, 1994).

Together with their industrial disengagement, the commercial banks did not attract enough deposits, preferring financial savings to deposits and commissions to interests (Gueslin, 1992). The introduction of deposit banks, like Crédit Industriel et Commercial and Crédit Lyonnais meant - unlike the Swedish development - increasing distance between bankers and entrepreneurs, even an aversion against industrial banking (Kindleberger, 1984, Patat, 1987).

The industrial disengagement of French commercial banks coincided with an increasing stock market capitalization during the 1880-1913 period (Gueslin, 1992). This indicates a shift from a credit-based financial system to a capital market-based financial system, i.e. from the bank convention to the bond convention. Freedeman (1993) argues that the extensive use of capital markets was a means for the banks to protect their own liquidity through the underwriting of bonds and shares. According to Gueslin (1992), the savings flow went outside the banks whose preferences had a bias toward foreign securities rather than industrial securities. Consequently, the overall picture suggests that France had, in the early 20th century, a strong bond convention.

Swedish commercial banks thrived in a relatively free financial system, a freedom that promoted economic growth (Sandberg, 1978, Sejersted, 1988). There was free entry into banking until 1911 (Larsson and Lindgren, 1992). Swedish banks were successful in attracting deposits, something which allowed more credit, reflected in a high ratio of financial assets to GNP, much higher in Sweden than in France (Sandberg, 1978).[7] Stockholms Enskilda Bank, Skandinaviska Banken, and Svenska Handelsbanken built up their industrial groups during the rapid industrialization 1890-1920 (Glete, 1994).

Banking was, however, sophisticated by 1870, before the rapid industrialization, and the population was educated enough to accept modern financial institutions and procedures (Sandberg, 1978, 1979). In fact, the Swedish banking system was an endowment contradicting the Coase theorem.[8] Institutions did not evolve to respond to need, because they existed already.

Merchant houses, which had dominated industrial finance until the 1890s, were no longer able to satisfy the demand for venture capital of the expanding industry, so the banks differentiated into underwriting of industrial bonds and shares as well as industrial reorganization (Lindgren, 1990). The banks expanded lending rapidly through lending on shares to finance entire development blocks, something they financed through borrowing from foreign banks and expansion of bank equity as deposits became insufficient to sustain the credit expansion (Nygren, 1983). Hence, the Swedish banks used the financial markets in Sweden and abroad to take over the position as industrial financiers and to establish durable links with industry. This suggests that a strong bank convention was established in Sweden in the early 20th century.

The commercial banks became the predominant industrial financiers in the 1890s and got the right to supply venture capital directly as industrial shareholders in 1911, a capacity expanded by indirect shareholding through associated issuing companies set up and funded by the banks, but liquidated during the 1920s when the banks took over the collateral shares (Lindgren, 1990, and Larsson and Lindgren, 1992). During World War I, Sweden had become a net exporter of capital, because exports had surged, something which pushed up share prices as well as lending against shares (Lundström, 1994). When capital imports had ceased to be an important activity, industrial client relationships became an important asset (Larsson and Lindgren, 1992). As a consequence of the recession in the early 1920s, banks took over shares from borrowers who defaulted (Lundström, 1994).

In France, however, the *banques d'affaires*, such as Paribas, involved themselves in industry (Bellon, 1980). Close ties with Paribas and Belgian banks meant that the steel company Forges et Acières du Nord et de l'Est was able to use the capital markets extensively rather than relying on retentions as source of finance (Freedeman, 1993).

Nevertheless, stock market capitalization declined during the interwar years when public and quasi-public institutions became more important as business financiers compared to commercial banks. According to Gueslin (1992), the ratio of stock market capitalization to national income declined from 2.78 in 1913 to 1.24 in 1937, while the business finance of the Caisse des Dépôts, Crédit Agricole, and Crédit National increased from 3.1 per cent of the commercial banks' business finance in 1920 to 38.9 per cent in 1938. The *banques d'affaires* were, however, active in the creation of corporations and industrial groups, but in 1918 only the steel industry was characterized by bank-industry groups and alliances (Bellon, 1980).

In Belgium, where industrial banking had been established well before Crédit Mobilier in France, banking became characterized by universal banks increasingly involved in industry through subsidiary specialized holdings in different industries (Kurgan-van Hentenryk, 1992). In France, however, industrial banking meant specialization, thus excluding many big banks.

The continuous and increasing industrial involvement of Swedish commercial banks suggests that the Swedish banking system was a sufficient institutional endowment, giving high network utilities, so bank-industry networks evolved spontaneously. The industrial disengagement of French commercial banks, gradually separated from the industrially involved *banques d'affaires*, suggests that the French banking system was an insufficient institutional endowment, giving low network utilities. The spontaneous evolution started, but failed, so collective action through public and quasi-public financial institutions emerged.

Hence, the bank convention was strong enough in Sweden, but too weak in France, to allow a spontaneous evolution of bank-industry networks. Yet, the choice between industrial involvement and industrial disengagement may be explained by differences in network commitment, i.e. differences in the institutional endowment effect, k, and the network duration effect, c.

Industrial involvement by banks within a bank-industry network requires mutual trust and network commitment between banker and entrepreneur. I will argue that Swedish banks based their industrial involvement on a banker-entrepreneur interaction characterized by mutual trust and network commitment, while the French banks' industrial disengagement was a consequence of a banker-entrepreneur interaction based on distrust and reluctance to commitment.

The reason is that network commitment as a moral commitment rule creates an institutional endowment which yields high trust, thus making a spontaneous evolution possible. This argument is related to Fukuyama's (1995) distinction between high-trust societies with spontaneous sociability and low-trust societies where sociability beyond the family level requires state support. Consequently, big business evolved spontaneously in high-trust societies, such as Japan, Germany, the USA before the decline of trust, and Sweden, while state support was necessary in the low-trust society of France.

In terms of my theoretical model, high-trust societies have a positive institutional endowment effect, k, provided banking is developed, and a high network duration effect, c, while low-trust societies have a non-positive institutional endowment effect, k, even when banking is developed, and a low network duration effect, c.

Network commitment and high trust create economic benefits of moral values. The high information intensity in Japan is possible because of loyalty and commitment (Whitley, 1990). Network commitment was of special importance for a late industrialized country, such as Sweden. In 1870, Sweden was poor compared to France and even poorer compared to Belgium whose industrialization had occurred early. Belgian industrial banking provided a model of investment banking in Sweden (Nilsson, 1981).

In terms of social capital, defined by Coleman (1988) as the ability to work together on the basis of shared values, Sweden was wealthier, as reflected in the strength of association liberalism. Social capital sustains human capital (Coleman, 1988) and may explain Sandberg's (1979) characterization of Sweden as an impoverished sophisticate in the mid 19th century, having a very high stock of human capital for its low income level. According to Fukuyama (1995), the absolute monarchy had destroyed the capacity for spontaneous sociability in France.

Why did French commercial banks avoid risks? Why did Kindleberger (1984) characterize the French financial system as backward? The anti-bank attitude was very strong. John Law's Mississippi Bubble in 1720 has already been mentioned. In addition, there was a tradition of hoarding. The *assignats*, the fiduciary state notes which collapsed in 1795, had induced hoarding (Davies, 1994). The banking crisis of 1930-31, when the Banque Adam and the Banque Nationale de Crédit failed, created public distrust, resulting in hoarding, so that the ratio of bank deposits to GNP fell from 0.32 in 1913 to 0.25 in 1938 (Gueslin, 1992).

This general public distrust seemed reflected in the banker-entrepreneur interaction. French banks supplied short-term credit to large, well-managed industrial corporations with a good profitability record, but long-term credit was considered too risky, while industrial corporations themselves, favoring retentions or sometimes securities as sources of finance, preferred short-term loans to long-term loans, in order to avoid the bankers as directors as well as the debt costs' adding to fixed costs (Freedeman, 1993). This suggests that the bankers were inclined to prefer an arm's length strategy and the entrepreneurs an unreliable strategy, since network commitment was too low to sustain a close relationship based on mutual trust.

Yet, there were some islands of mutual trust and network commitment before World War I. The banks of Meurthe et Moselle provided industrial enterprises with credit initially, later turned into bonds as the business succeeded, thus maintaining a regional financial market of industrial securities (Gueslin, 1992). Forges et Acières du Nord et de l'Est with its banks represented in the board, used bank loans as source of finance during its early history in the 1880s, but relied heavily on securities after the turn of the century (Freedeman, 1993).

During the interwar years, however, the big banks preferred government securities to such an extent that bank credit became less important in relation to national income in the late 1930s than it had been before 1914, thereby increasing the importance of retentions as source of finance for industrial corporations (Gueslin, 1992). This indicates that the bankers did not trust the entrepreneurs very much, but preferred riskfree investments. French bankers had a low network commitment, the *banques d'affaires* being the exception.

In Sweden, there was a higher degree of mutual trust between bankers and entrepreneurs. Skandinaviska Banken had three regional boards with its industrial clients in each region as members, thus maintaining cooperative relations with industrial corporations and their owners, while Svenska Handelsbanken's relations with industry was organized as an executive coalition (Glete, 1994).

Stockholms Enskilda Bank of the Wallenberg group combined ownership, entrepreneurial, and creditor functions and was represented in the boards of its industrial clients, but in cooperative relations very far from principal-agent relations (Lindgren, 1990). Stockholms Enskilda Bank was founded along Scottish lines, the preferred model of the association liberals whose liberalism, being very influential in Sweden from 1820 to 1870, had cooperation between individuals within voluntary associations and natural development as key elements (Nilsson, 1981). Hence, network-orientation was consistent with Swedish attitudes.

Swedish entrepreneurs preferred informed bankers, avoiding banks playing an arm's length strategy. After World War II, Götabanken - an arm's length banker - had very few big industrial clients, since its industrial competence was questioned, while the other big banks, Skandinaviska Banken, Svenska Handelsbanken, and Stockholms Enskilda Bank, maintained stable groups, as informed bankers (Glete, 1994). This indicates that entrepreneurs were inclined to network commitment.

A similar inclination to network commitment can be seen among Swedish bankers. The financial superstar Ivar Kreuger and his multinational match-based industrial group of the 1920s provides an illustrative example. Skandinaviska Kreditaktiebolaget, as Skandinaviska Banken was then called, was by far the largest creditor of Kreuger's Swedish match company, Svenska Tändsticks Aktiebolaget, and trusted Kreuger so much that control measures proposed by Svenska Handelsbanken in 1923 were rejected (Hildebrand, 1985). This indicates a resolute behavior of network commitment. The death of Kreuger in 1932 led eventually to the crash of the Kreuger group. This was obviously a set-back for Skandinaviska Banken as network banker, but it did not shift from an informed strategy to an arm's length one. The industrial sphere of Skandinaviska Banken remained stable from the 1920s to the 1970s (Glete, 1994).

The lack of mutual trust between bankers and entrepreneurs in France, reflected in a shift to arm's length relations, except for the *banques d'affaires*, suggests that network commitment was an insufficient institutional endowment for industrially involved banks in France, so the commercial banks disengaged. The stability of Swedish bank-industry networks, their cooperative nature, and the entrepreneurs' preference for informed bankers indicate that network commitment was a sufficient institutional endowment for industrially involved banks in Sweden.

4.5 Swedish Upper Bounds vs. French Fully Privileged Groups: Collective Action and the Spontaneous Evolution

By 1930, bank-industry groups had evolved spontaneously in Sweden, but failed to do so in France. Collective action was, however, implemented differently in the two countries. In Sweden, bank ownership of industrial shares became in 1934 prohibited in principle, thus putting an upper limit to the spontaneous evolution, a bank convention with upper bounds. A maximum institutional endowment effect, k, was imposed. In France, the growing importance of public and quasi-public financial institutions, leading to a state-coordinated financial system after World War II, meant that bank-industry networks were established by collective action favoring the bank convention. As low-trust society, France had a non-positive institutional endowment effect, k, and a low network duration effect, c. Bank-industry networks were, therefore, made fully privileged.

After Sweden's legislative ban on the banks' being industrial shareholders in 1934 - a consequence of the crash of the Kreuger group - the banks resorted to indirect shareholding through associated investment companies, Investor and Providentia of Stockholms Enskilda Bank, Custos and later Säfveån of Skandinaviska Banken, and Industrivärden of Svenska Handelsbanken (Thunholm, 1989, Larsson and Lindgren, 1992).

The group around Svenska Handelsbanken was made very strong from the early 1960s through cross-ownership between Industrivärden and the forestry company SCA which the bank had created together with Ivar Kreuger in 1929 (Glete, 1994). Larsson and Lindgren (1992) argue that the associated investment companies meant that permanent banking groups with close bank-industry links were established.

The bank-industry networks were preserved through affiliated investment companies, but the latter reflected the higher link maintenance costs imposed through legislation. One would expect smaller benefits from the bank convention, but the bond convention was not given much opportunity until the 1980s. In order to combine cheap money and low inflation, the government kept the financial system regulated during the 1950-1985 period (Larsson, 1995). As of 1985, financial markets expanded with increasing arm's length financing, including multiple bank contacts, weaker connection between the ownership and creditor functions, and increased mobility between main banks (Berglöf and Sjögren, 1995). An interesting research issue for further research would be to study the extent to which Swedish bank-industry networks were preserved through affiliated investment companies as a consequence of the regulated financial system during the 1950-1985 period. Nevertheless, Swedish collective action seems to have put upper bounds on the bond convention as well as the bank convention through a minimum institutional endowment effect, k.

The legal separation of the ownership and creditor functions, nevertheless, decreased the hard core of the Wallenberg group where Stockholms Enskilda Bank maintained creditor, ownership, and managerial functions (Lindgren, 1990). The bank became less important within the group whose orientation shifted from finance to industry (Glete, 1994). The bank-industry networks were preserved through the bank-associated investment companies, although with more complicated and expensive links. According to Lindgren (1994), the Wallenberg family maintained the close links between the bank and the investment companies until 1982. For Svenska Handelsbanken, the links between the bank and its investment company, Industrivärden were merely historical and personal (Hildebrand, 1971). The group was made strong through the cross-ownership between Industrivärden and SCA (Glete, 1994). This suggests that the Swedish Stag Hunt game was characterized by rather high network utilities, although lower after World War II than in the 1920s.

The French mercantilist and protectionist tradition was in the postwar period reflected in a state-sponsored capitalism where the financial system was organized in a complex structure of financial circuits, as an instrument for state intervention, until the mid 1960s (Zysman, 1983, Green, 1986). Industrial banking was implemented by the *banques d'affaires*, such as Paribas and Suez. The Suez group, having its origins in the financing of the Suez canal, performed entrepreneurial as well as creditor functions (Bonin, 1987). The *banques d'affaires*, however, had more limited funds than the commercial banks, something which was not a problem before 1945 when French firms were rather small (Zysman, 1983).

Learning-by-financing on a large scale was not really possible until the postwar period when the government changed the institutional dynamics through collective action. This was implemented with the Trésor of the Ministry of Finance as the bank of the economy controlling the bond market and the Banque de France as price and quantity setter at the money market, while a link was established between the government and the banking system through the National Credit Council (Conceil National du Crédit), using the Crédit National to induce the banks to commit themselves to long-term industrial lending (Zysman, 1983).

In fact, the government designed bank-industry networks as privileged groups, using the Trésor as the supernetwork bank of the French economy with the National Credit Council and Crédit National as permanent members of the bank-industry networks. The bank convention was the only ESS in the postwar game, at least until 1966 when the commercial banks and the *banques d'affaires* were allowed to combine equity holding and commercial banking. This legislation yielded not only a considerably higher supply of credit to meet the investment-induced demand, but also a decentralization of the financial system away from the Trésor at the center to the banks at the periphery (Zysman, 1983, Patat, 1987).

Collective action shifted into the direction of spontaneous order. As a result of the new legislation, the *banques d'affaires* were able to use deposits to refinance their industrial banking and the national commercial banks to diversify into investment banking. Bank-industry networks, therefore, became possible on a larger scale without having the Trésor as a superbank designing the networks.

The French state, thus, increased the involvement of banks in industry, while the Swedish state put limitations on the banks' industrial involvement, but seems to have done so also to the capital market. France, had gone from a Fully Privileged Stag Hunt game under collective action to a Stag Hunt game with some spontaneous order in its process of strengthening the bank convention, while Sweden got an upper limit on the network utilities of its Stag Hunt game and thereby a bank convention with upper bounds. However, Swedish collective action seems to have put lower limits on the network utilities as well and thereby a bond convention with upper bounds.

4.6 Summary

My purpose was to show how bank-industry networks, based on mutual trust and network commitment, evolve spontaneously due to learning-by-financing only when the institutional endowments - network commitment and developed banking - are sufficient, and that some collective action might be necessary to make the spontaneous evolution of bank-industry networks feasible. Bank-industry networks may evolve spontaneously, following the Smith-Menger-Hayek conjecture, or trough collective action, along the Olson-Buchanan-Tullock conjecture. The former is entirely based on function and social interaction, while the latter involves intention and the design of fully privileged groups.

Analyzing Schumpeterian banker-entrepreneur interaction as an evolutionary Stag Hunt game, I provide a functionalist-evolutionary explanation of why bank-industry networks exist in a world with uncertainty and bounded rationality. The evolutionary game gives two evolutionary stable strategies, corresponding to the two spontaneously evolved conventions of industrial innovation finance: (i) the bank convention with bankers and entrepreneurs cooperating within bank-industry networks and (ii) the bond convention with independent bankers and entrepreneurs.

Along each quality ladder of the economy, bankers and entrepreneurs play for each innovation a two-person random pairing game between a member of the population of bankers and a member of the population of entrepreneurs. As there is behavioral uncertainty, bankers and entrepreneurs may meet again without remembering the behavioral strategy of the other player.

The shares of network bankers and network entrepreneurs are assumed to be random at the initial stage of each game, so for each vintage of innovations the networks are reborn. Learning-by-financing built up around the old vintage of innovations may be relevant or irrelevant for the new one in a random fashion. The institutional dynamics of the game gives, therefore, the probabilities of convergence to the bank convention and bond convention, respectively. As vintages of innovations are assumed to arrive frequently, thus shaking up the process of institutional change, the institutional dynamics make the financial system an evolving combination of the bank convention and the bond convention.

The older and more viable the networks and the higher their complexity and network commitment, the higher the learning-by-financing becomes. Hence, the network utilities increase, thus making the bank convention stronger in the economy.

Bank-industry networks evolve spontaneously only when the institutional endowments - network commitment and developed banking - are sufficient, otherwise some collective action might be necessary to make the bank convention feasible through the design of bank-industry networks as fully privileged groups. The historical evolution of bank-industry networks can be explained by spontaneous order in Sweden, while such an order failed in France.

A historical analysis indicates that the banking system and the network commitment were sufficient institutional endowments in Sweden, thus making the bank convention viable. In France, however, banking and network commitment were insufficient as institutional endowments, so the bank convention was not viable. The French bank-industry networks evolved through collective action by the French government, making the bank convention fully privileged, while Swedish collective action was aimed at putting upper bounds on the bank convention, but tended to do so on the bond convention as well.

Main Symbols

α: utility of informed bankers (network bankers)
ω: utility of reliable entrepreneurs (network entrepreneurs)
p: share of informed bankers (network bankers) in the population of bankers
q: share of reliable entrepreneurs (network entrepreneurs) in the population of entrepreneurs
N(t): realization of new information through learning-by-financing at time t
d_i: required duration of network link for the ith arrival of information through learning-by-financing
t_{max}: life time of a vintage of innovations
α_i: utility of informed bankers (network bankers) who have achieved the ith level of learning-by-financing
ω_i: utility of reliable entrepreneurs (network entrepreneurs) at the ith level of learning-by-financing
s_i: share of the ith level of learning-by-financing among network bankers and entrepreneurs
d^A, d^B, d^C: durations of the link between the banker and entrepreneurs A, B, and C, respectively
c: network commitment between entrepreneurs
θ_A: banker's learning-by-financing about entrepreneur A
E_i: ratio of bank convention entrepreneurial rents to bond convention entrepreneurial rents at the ith level of learning-by-financing
R_i: ratio of bank convention interest payments to bond convention interest payments at the ith level of learning-by-financing
k: public utility within the network due to institutional endowments (network commitment between banker and entrepreneur and developed

banking) when the private utility is set to one
σ: banker's share of entrepreneur's equity

Notes

1. Sections 4.1 through 4.3 extend the analysis in Marmefelt (1998) of Schumpeterian banker-entrepreneur interaction as an evolutionary Stag Hunt game, where I show that the spontaneous evolution of bank-industry networks depends on institutional endowments, such as developed banking and network commitment. Sections 4.4 and 4.5 use the historical analysis in Marmefelt (1997).

2. See e.g. Ullmann-Margalit (1977), Schotter (1981), Axelrod (1984), and Sugden (1986) who all use game theory to explain the evolution of institutions or rules.

3. See e.g. Langlois (1986) for a comparison between functional explanations focusing on why institutions exist and causal-genetic explanations focusing on how they have emerged. Although both are valuable, the former opens up for a comparison between spontaneous order and collective action through the connection between function and intention.

4. Sugden's definition is, therefore, broader than the one used by Lewis (1969) which is limited to established conventions. For Sugden it is sufficient that everyone conform and expect everyone else to conform to a regularity of behavior, but Lewis requires in addition that everyone conforms on condition that the others do. Hence, following Sugden, a convention may arise in other than coordination games.

5. An ESS fulfills two conditions: (i) being the best response to itself and (ii) being uninvadable.

6. The endowment effect of sellers' reservation price being higher than the one of the buyers contradicts the Coase theorem by saying that initial property rights are not neutral (Kahneman, Knetch and Thaler (1990). Bankers and entrepreneurs of a bank-industry network have initial institutional endowments, such as developed banking and network commitment between banker and entrepreneur, yielding a network-specific utility.

7. According to Sandberg (1978), the ratio of assets of all financial institutions to GNP was 0.89 for Sweden and 0.50 for France in 1880, increasing to 1.36 for Sweden and 1.04 for France in 1913.

8. Kindleberger (1984) argues that Sweden did not contradict the Coase theorem, because the merchant houses were important in industrial finance, but Sweden had

before its industrialization a strong banking system, creating a high growth potential.

5 The Viability of Bank-Industry Networks in a Securitized Economy: An Assessment of Structural Changes in the Institutional Dynamics of Banker-Entrepreneur Interaction

5.1 Assessing the Viability of the Bank Convention

The securitized economy which evolved during the 1980s has increased competition in banking. According to OECD (1992), this development led to overcapacity in corporate banking, because large industrial enterprises have internalized industrial banking. On the one hand, banks have very low rates of return on corporate lending, but universal banks have, on the other hand, become very active in securities services.

In chapter 3, I showed that a bank-industry network may yield a higher innovativeness due to the banker's learning-by-financing within the network. If bank-industry networks produce perfect learning-by-financing in the bank convention, while there is no learning-by-financing due to the non-existence of bank-industry networks in the bond convention, then the bank convention yields growth regimes with higher innovativeness than the bond convention.

In chapter 4, I analyzed Schumpeterian banker-entrepreneur interaction as an evolutionary Stag Hunt game to show how bank-industry networks evolve either through spontaneous order or collective action. Furthermore, I explained the evolution of bank-industry networks by spontaneous order in Sweden and by collective action in France. The relative fitness of the bank convention in the evolutionary selection process increases with the network payoffs which are dependent on network commitment through the institutional endowment effect and the network duration effect. If network commitment is strong, then there would be no need for collective action designing bank-industry networks.

My purpose in this chapter is to study institutional change in the financial systems during the 1980s by linking the theoretical analysis above with the analysis in chapter 2 of the evolutionary viability of the universal bank and the bank convention in a securitized economy.

An assessment of industrial finance conventions according to their liquidity and solvency will be made to analyze whether the system differences in the payoff structure of the evolutionary Stag Hunt game in chapter 4 has declined with the evolution of the securitized economy. Has network commitment decreased, thus reducing the network payoffs through the institutional endowment effect and the network duration effect? If that were the case, then the bond convention would become dominant for all financial systems.

For empirical studies, Japan has a very strong bank convention, while the USA has a very strong bond convention. One should, however, bear in mind that the Japanese main bank system had its heyday during the 1951-75 period and turned more market-embedded after 1975 (Aoki, Patrick, and Sheard, 1994), while there are innovative networks around venture capitalists in the USA (Langlois and Robertson, 1995). This gives a strong bank convention with long network durations in Japan and a weak bank convention with short network durations in the USA. Sweden and France are in between Japan and the USA, as countries with a rather strong bank convention, but where the bond convention might have increased its strength due to financial market expansion during the 1980s.

There is a central question at issue: How have Swedish and French industrial finance systems developed in relation the Japanese and American ones during the 1982-90 period?

This period is of special interest, because it covers the securitization process without being affected by the financial crisis of the 1990s which was the consequence of real estate speculation. A financial crisis tends to reduce network commitment, at least temporarily, but it is still too early to say whether the financial crisis of the 1990s has permanently reduced network commitment.

Important indicators in my analysis are liquidity and solvency, gross and net sources of finance, macroeconomic ratios of broad money to GDP and claims of the banking sector on the non-financial private sector to GDP together with the debt/equity ratio, as well as ratios of financial investment to non-financial investment, short-term debt to long-term debt, and retentions to gross trading profit. An analysis of industrial finance conventions, liquidity, and solvency has been developed by Rivaud-Danset and Salais (1992) for four different conventions. As we shall see, my bank convention and bond convention may be analyzed in a similar way. A high liquidity combined with a low solvency indicates a strong bank convention, and a high solvency combined with a low liquidity a strong bond convention. The network specific payoffs of the evolutionary Stag Hunt game will be high in the former case and low in the latter.

According to earlier empirical studies (McCauley and Zimmer, 1989, and Zimmer and McCauley, 1991), Japan had a lower cost of capital for industrial R&D projects with a 10 year payoff lag as well as a lower cost of equity in banking than the USA. This should then be reflected in the financing of industry. For this purpose, I will analyze the gross and net sources of finance of non-financial enterprises, like Mayer (1988, 1990) and Mayer and Alexander (1990), but from a different perspective. Their reasoning is essentially based on principal-agent inspired control rights, while my approach is based on the difference in network commitment and thereby in mutual trust between industrial finance conventions, because the cost of control is too high, given the uncertainty of the innovation process and bounded rationality.

My theoretical analysis in chapter 3 suggests that a strong bank convention implies a greater importance of loans as financing source, because debt increases with learning-by-financing. At the macroeconomic level, indicators of financial development of King and Levine (1993) - the ratio of broad money to GDP and the ratio of claims of the banking sector on the non-financial private sector to GDP - could be used. A strong bank convention would increase the ratio of broad money to GDP and the ratio of claims on the non-financial private sector to GDP. On the balance sheets of industrial firms, this would increase the debt/equity ratio and the bank loans' share of total liabilities. Yet, industrial firms may internalize the banking function with the firm working as a kind of financial holding. The higher the ratio of financial investment to non-financial investment, the more the industrial firms perform the banking function themselves, leading to borrowing beyond what the strength of the bank convention justifies.

Bearing this in mind, the trust the banks have in the innovative skills of the industrial client firms is reflected in the ratio of short-term debt to long-term debt of the industrial firms. Short-term loans provide a means to meet the periodic surges of cash requirements during the innovation process (OECD, 1995). According to the bank convention, the high liquidity may be achieved through short-term bank credits. These do not give any control rights to the banks. Hence, the creditors' trust in their industrial clients is higher when they supply more credit with a larger share being short-term. Furthermore, the industrial firms are more autonomous when the ratio of retentions to gross trading profit is high. Creditors have more trust when they supply more credit without decreasing this autonomy. The more important loans as source of finance in relation to the ratio of retentions to gross trading profit, the greater the creditors' trust is.

In the following sections, these indicators will be used, starting with the commitment to bank-industry networks in the evolving securitized economy, in section 5.2. This leads in section 5.3 to an assessment of industrial finance conventions, liquidity, and solvency. Section 5.4 considers the network approach and its stressing network commitment and trust rather than control. Finally, section 5.5 gives a summary.

5.2 The Commitment to Bank-Industry Networks in the Evolving Securitized Economy of the 1980s

As long as the banks are able to maintain their client firms within the network by diversifying their services, the securitized economy imposes no threat to learning-by-financing. The high capacity of universal banks to diversify have made the universal banking system diffuse throughout the industrialized world, but the increasing financial fragility as the banks have riskier portfolios put a limit to diversification, calling for some respecialization to cut costs (OECD, 1992). This respecialization should, however, be seen as an adjustment, where banks give up some specialized activities to avoid a profit squeeze. Bank learning-by-financing still has an important role to play together with guarantee and back-up facilities. Consequently, a higher share of bank profits is expected to come from commissions and fees and a lower share from interest rate margins (OECD, 1992). Hence, bank-industry networks prevail with a new bank-market combination, where the banks intermediate securitized debt through the back-up and guarantee facilities to their client companies.

Using macroeconomic financial indicators, King and Levine (1993) who work within the tradition of cross-country empirical studies of growth,[1] find that finance matters to economic growth. Their study is based on a cross section of about 80 countries for the 1960-89 period. Indicators of the level of financial development, such as financial depth (the ratio of broad money to GDP) or the ratio of claims on the non-financial private sector to GDP, were strongly correlated with economic growth, the rate of physical capital accumulation, and the improvements in the efficiency of capital during the 1960-89 period.

What King and Levine consider as indicators of the level of financial development might as well be indicators of the strength of the bank convention. My theoretical analysis implies that a strong bank convention reflects a larger role of the banking system in the economy. The ratio of money plus quasi-money to GDP (M2/GDP) and the ratio of claims of the banking system (central bank and commercial banks) on the non-financial private sector to GDP should be higher. These two ratios represent two aspects of the same phenomenon. The money supply reflects deposits and thereby bank lending to the private sector. In the securitized economy, however, bonds play a larger role as a close substitute for money. Hence, the ratio of claims on the non-financial private sector to GDP might be higher than the ratio of money plus quasi-money to GDP.

Table 5.1 shows that over the 1982-90 period, Japan had a higher ratio of broad money to GDP (M2/GDP) than the USA. France was in between, but Sweden had a lower ratio than the USA. The ratio of claims on the non-financial private sector shows a similar pattern, according to Table 5.2.

A problem of the macroeconomic indicators are, of course, their roughness. The private sector does not sort out households from non-financial enterprises. Let us, therefore, turn to the firm-level of non-financial corporations. By focusing on industry, a better assessment of industrial finance conventions is possible.

Table 5.3 shows how the differences in industry debt/equity ratios were still substantial between the systems with Japanese firms relying heavily on debt at one end of the spectrum and American firms on equity at the other end. French and Swedish firms were in between. These differences indicates the strength of the bank convention in Japan and of the bond convention in the USA.

Table 5.1 Ratio of Money plus Quasi-Money to GDP

	Japan	France	Sweden	USA
1982	0.88	0.68	0.48	0.54
1983	0.91	0.68	0.49	0.57
1984	0.90	0.68	0.51	0.57
1985	0.92	0.68	0.50	0.58
1986	0.96	0.68	0.50	0.61
1987	1.02	0.69	0.51	0.61
1988	1.05	0.68	0.50	0.59
1989	1.09	0.66	0.49	0.58
1990	1.12	0.64	0.47	0.57

Source: IMF International Financial Statistics, 1992.

Table 5.2 Ratio of Claims on the Private Sector to GDP of Monetary Authorities and Deposit Money Banks

	Japan	France	Sweden	USA
1982	0.86	0.71	0.41	0.61
1983	0.90	0.72	0.40	0.61
1984	0.92	0.74	0.38	0.62
1985	0.95	0.75	0.38	0.64
1986	1.00	0.76	0.39	0.67
1987	1.06	0.81	0.42	0.70
1988	1.10	0.86	0.47	0.71
1989	1.15	0.88	0.52	0.71
1990	1.18	0.92	0.56	0.69

Source: IMF International Financial Statistics, 1992.

Table 5.3 Debt/Equity Ratios of Non-Financial Corporations

	Japan[1]	France[2]	Sweden	USA
1982	5.02	2.61	2.01	0.46
1983	4.84	2.65	1.88	0.49
1984	4.77	2.53	1.88	0.54
1985	4.40	2.39	1.87	0.58
1986	4.22	2.05	1.89	0.64
1987	4.36	1.76	1.75	0.70
1988	4.19	1.64	1.81	0.75
1989	4.04	1.45	1.98	0.78
1990	4.00	1.37	2.03	0.82

Notes:
1. Total sample.
2. Industrial firms.

Source: OECD Financial Statistics III: Non-Financial Enterprises Financial Statements, 1990 and 1992.

The Japanese keiretsu is the most outstanding bank-industry network. The access to short-term credit is an important source of liquidity (Salais and Rivaud-Danset, 1992). The ratio of short-term debt on the liability side is met by a high ratio of cash and deposits at the asset side (Aoki, 1988). Empirical studies suggest that liquidity does not impose a constraint on investment for the keiretsu firms (Hoshi, Kashyap, and Scharfstein, 1991) and that Japan has a lower cost of capital for industrial R&D projects with a 10 year payoff lag than the USA (McCauley and Zimmer, 1989). According to McCauley and Zimmer (1989), the cost of capital is low in Japan, because the keiretsu reduces risk. Becchetti (1995) finds that stable shareholders and strong bank-industry links seem to reduce the differences between the costs of external financing and the costs of internal financing.

The arm's length market-oriented American system provides a striking contrast. Financial intermediaries in the USA make very poor assessments of risk with insufficient risk premia (Artus, 1990). The results of McCauley and Zimmer (1989) suggest that American firms may not increase their debt/equity ratios to Japanese levels without becoming much more financially fragile. The high learning-by-financing of the Japanese keiretsu allows for high debt/equity ratios at low costs of capital and maintained stability.

The extremely high debt/equity ratios in Japan might, however, be explained by off-balance sheet assets, the compensating balance the bank requires its client firm to keep in the bank, and the importance of trade credits (Aoki, 1988). The compensating balance creates strong ties between the bank and the industrial firm, so the firm may build up its high cash ratio through short-term credit from the bank. Aoki stresses the bargaining power of the bank, but can also be explained as a mechanism for maintaining the network commitment.

By considering the bank loans' share of total liabilities, one would exclude the effect of trade credits. The OECD Financial Statistics does, however, not always distinguish banks from other institutions. Loans are given for financial institutions in Japan where most of them are banks and for banks and others in Sweden. Table 5.4 gives, nevertheless, an approximation of the importance of bank loans for total liabilities. The differences are sufficiently considerable to maintain the picture that banks are much more important for industrial firms in Japan than in the USA with Sweden and France in between. Japanese banks seem to have maintained their position, while French banks have declined in importance during the

1980s.

In Japan, the stronghold for the bank convention, the keiretsu banks have exploited the possibilities created by the expanding financial markets, making securitization into a shift from bank loans to a combination of loans and securities supplied by banks. Japanese banks have used securities to remain the main external financing source (Gerlach, 1992). Firms with very good performance have increased their freedom within the relationship to their main banks, but the latter remain exclusive monitors (Aoki, Patrick, and Sheard, 1994).

The French financial system has changed dramatically during the 1980s. Capital markets, encouraged by collective action, have expanded rapidly with disintermediation as a natural consequence (Patat, 1987). Competition between intermediated and non-intermediated sources of finance has increased through government measures. Illustrative examples are the Delors Law of 1983, allowing instruments, such as floating-rate bonds, convertible bonds, bonds with warrants, investment certificates, and participating shares, the creation of venture capital funds, *fonds communs de placement à risques*, as well as the establishment of the *second marché* (Bisignano, 1992).

In addition, French banks have lost two important sources of short-term assets when the commercial papers were introduced in 1985 and the banking system's monopoly on treasury-bill trading was abolished in 1986. The banks have, however, responded to the challenge. Securitization of loans was made feasible through the *fonds communs de créances* set up in 1988 (Beduc et al, 1992, Bisignano, 1992). Securities houses which were earlier family owned are now subsidiaries of banks (Beduc et al, 1992). As institutional investors, French banks have built up strong links with industry as well as insurance companies (Pastré, 1992).

Yet one may observe that there was a larger decline in bank loans as share of total liabilities during the five year period following the introduction the commercial paper in France from 27.8% in 1985 to 20.3% in 1989, while the decline was smaller after the introduction the commercial paper in Sweden from 24.2% 1983 to 19.9% in 1987. Later bank loans increased in Sweden.

Table 5.4 Bank Loans as Share of Total Liabilities of Non-Financial Corporations (in percent)

	Japan[1]	France[2]	Sweden[3]	USA
1982	39.3	29.9	24.9	6.4
1983	39.3	29.1	24.2	6.6
1984	39.3	29.7	23.3	7.4
1985	39.0	27.4	21.9	7.6
1986	40.4	26.2	21.1	8.1
1987	40.9	23.4	19.9	7.9
1988	39.6	21.7	23.9	8.0
1989	37.8	20.3	22.7	8.2
1990	40.6	20.4	21.3	8.4

Notes:
1. Total sample. Loans from financial institutions.
2. Industrial enterprises. Short-term loans from banks + long-term borrowing.
3. Loans from banks and others.

Source: OECD Financial Statistics III: Non-Financial Enterprises Financial Statements, 1990 and 1992.

The Swedish banks seem to have kept their positions better than the French ones. Nevertheless, the Swedish picture is one of a rapid money market expansion during the 1980s with a shift towards securities, and bank diversification (Sveriges Riksbank, 1991). Money market instruments, such as treasury bills, certificates of deposit, and commercial papers were introduced in Sweden 1980-83, somewhat earlier than the French 1985-86 introduction period (OECD 1989a). A rapid financial market expansion has moved the Swedish financial system towards a market-oriented one, but the bank-affiliated investment companies have strengthened their ownership positions within their respective network (Berglöf, 1988). Corporate bonds have, furthermore, been intermediated by banks (Thunholm, 1989). As of 1985, however, more diversified bank connections have developed and industrial firms have become more inclined to switch main bank (Berglöf and Sjögren, 1995). Increased competition for good clients followed the deregulation of the financial system, completed in 1986 (Larsson, 1995).

Nevertheless, banks do not perform the same learning-by-financing when the investment companies are the network coordinators. The bankers have weaker links with the entrepreneurs. In general, the Swedish banking system is universal, although there are e.g. specialized mortgage institutions. Swedish banks were, however, prohibited from being industrial equity shareholders - with some exceptions - during the post Kreuger era of Swedish industrial finance, 1934-91. This suggests relatively weak bank-industry networks in Sweden, so one would expect securitization to decrease the importance of bank loans. Securitization itself would give more market-embedded bank-industry networks of the kind Aoki, Patrick, and Sheard (1994) observe for Japan. Therefore, the industrial finance conventions and the financing of industry have to be considered.

5.3 An Assessment of Industrial Finance Conventions, Liquidity, Solvency, and Financing of Industry

At the macroeconomic level, the ratio of broad money to GDP might be seen as national liquidity and the ratio of claims on the non-financial private sector to GDP might be used to construct a national solvency indicator. Solvency would be the ratio of GDP to the sum of GDP and the claims on the non-financial private sector.

Yet, if one wants to analyze the liquidity and solvency of industrial enterprises, then firm-level indicators would be more appropriate. My data is coming from the OECD Financial Statistics III: Non-Financial Enterprises Financial Statements. Here, my purpose is to make an assessment of industrial finance conventions, by studying liquidity and solvency of non-financial corporations.

Rivaud-Danset and Salais (1992) have four different industrial finance conventions: (i) the financial market industrial convention, (ii) the contractual convention, (iii) the interpersonal convention, and (iv) the collective guarantee convention. The first of these conventions is a pure circular flow convention without uncertainty, but gradually uncertainty, the need for flexibility, and the relative importance of intangible assets increase for conventions (ii) through (iv).

As my analysis concerns innovation and entrepreneurship, the first convention is irrelevant. The contractual convention corresponds to my bond convention as the banker keeps arm's length distance, while the interpersonal convention and with collective action even the collective guarantee convention correspond to my bank convention. The network banker has trough learning-by-financing an interpersonal relationship with the network entrepreneurs, but in addition collective action provides collective guarantees within the bank-industry network for long-term innovation projects.

Rivaud-Danset and Salais (1992) analyze liquidity according to the transaction versus flexibility motive and solvency according to the accumulation motive. The interpersonal convention has higher liquidity - flexibility rather than transaction is the motive - but lower solvency than the contractual convention. As Rivaud-Danset and Salais (1992) correctly point out, high liquidity might be created both by retained earnings or short-term credit, but in the latter case which is common in Japan, standard corporate finance ratios would consider the firm relatively illiquid. This is rather absurd, as one advantage of the bank-industry network is its supplying credit to improve liquidity of the firms. Hoshi, Kashyap, and Scharfstein (1991) find for Japanese firms that investment was less liquidity sensitive for the firms with close financial ties to banks, i.e. the network firms where bank learning-by-financing is high.

In a Schumpeterian context, credit gives high liquidity which provides purchasing power to innovate, but higher debt decreases solvency. Hence, the bank convention, where learning-by-financing is strong and the higher debt/equity ratio higher, is characterized by higher liquidity and lower solvency than the bond convention. According to the bank convention, the informed network banks provide additional funds to the network firms which thereby become less constrained by the liquidity derived from retained earnings as compared to the independent firms of the bond convention.

As liquidity indicator I will, therefore, use a quick ratio where value added is substituted for current liabilities, i.e. the ratio of the sum of cash and deposits, short-term securities, and receivables, to value added, so that liquidity achieved through short-term debt is not discriminated. The ratio of equity to total liabilities then provides an indicator of solvency.

Table 5.5 shows that Japanese industrial firms had the highest liquidity followed by Swedish, French, and American firms whose liquidity is the lowest one. This suggests that the bank convention is strongest in Japan and weakest in the USA with Sweden and France in between. According to Table 5.6, solvency was highest for American and lowest for Japanese industrial firms, again with French firms, whose solvency increased, and Swedish firms in between.

The combinations of liquidity and solvency indicates that Sweden and France combined the bank and bond conventions in hybrid financial systems in between the bank convention-dominated Japan and the bond convention-dominated USA, although the bond convention became stronger in France.

My theoretical analysis implies that the stronger the bank convention, the better the learning-by-financing and the lower the costs of capital, because the banker's information costs are reduced. An empirical study by Becchetti (1995) suggests that the stable shareholders and strong bank-industry links of Japan tend to reduce the costs of external financing. Hence, loans would be relatively more important compared to retentions as financing source of industry, although banks may combine loans and securities in the securitized economy. An assessment of the financing of investment could be done through a comparison of gross and net sources of finance (Mayer 1988, 1990, and Mayer and Alexander, 1990).

Table 5.7 gives the gross and the net sources[2] of finance of Japanese, French, Swedish, and American non-financial corporations. The more dominant the bank convention, the more important loans are expected to be in comparison to retentions.

Table 5.5 Liquidity (ratio of cash & deposits + short-term securities + receivables to value added) of Non-Financial Corporations

	Japan[1]	Sweden	France[2]	USA[3]
1982	2.06	0.93	0.83	0.53
1983	2.08	0.92	0.89	0.55
1984	2.08	0.95	0.91	0.53
1985	2.03	0.94	0.92	0.52
1986	2.11	0.95	0.92	0.56
1987	2.19	0.96	0.90	0.55
1988	2.18	0.96	0.88	0.57
1989	2.29	0.87	0.89	0.57
1990	2.23	0.91	0.93	0.57

Notes:

1. Total sample. Value added includes capital gains/losses.
2. Industrial enterprises. Excludes other accounts receivable which are considered as short-term lending.
3. Excludes short-term government securities.

Source: OECD Financial Statistics III: Non-Financial Enterprises Financial Statements, 1990 and 1992.

Table 5.6 Solvency (ratio of equity to total liabilities) of Non-Financial Corporations

	Japan[1]	Sweden	France[2]	USA
1982	0.17	0.33	0.28	0.68
1983	0.17	0.35	0.27	0.67
1984	0.17	0.35	0.28	0.65
1985	0.19	0.35	0.29	0.63
1986	0.19	0.35	0.33	0.61
1987	0.19	0.36	0.36	0.59
1988	0.19	0.36	0.38	0.57
1989	0.20	0.34	0.41	0.56
1990	0.20	0.33	0.42	0.55

Notes:
1. Total sample.
2. Industrial firms.

Source: OECD Financial Statistics III: Non-Financial Enterprises Financial Statements, 1990 and 1992.

Table 5.7 Unweighted Average Financing of Non-Financial Corporations, 1982-90

Gross Sources of Finance
(in percent of total sources)

	Japan[1]	Sweden[2]	France[3]	USA
Retentions	39.6	43.7	44.7	72.2
Capital transfer	N.A.	0.1	0.4	0.0
Short-term securities & payables	14.8	18.0	14.0	8.6
Loans	34.3	32.9	26.0	11.9
Long-term securities	11.3	5.2	14.9	7.4
Total	100.0	99.9	100.0	100.1

Net Sources of Finance
(in percent of non-financial investment)

	Japan[1]	Sweden[2]	France[3]	USA
Retentions	65.0	108.1	94.6	96.2
Capital transfer	N.A.	0.1	0.8	0.0
Short-term securities & payables	-26.7	-1.3	-6.9	-11.1
Loans	56.9	27.6	36.0	15.1
Long-term securities	2.7	-34.1	-24.5	4.2
Statistical adjustment	2.0	-0.4	0.0	-4.3
Total	99.9	100.0	100.0	100.1

Notes:
1. Total sample.
2. Trade credits from/to affiliates are included in loans. Loans from affiliates were 17.8 percent as gross source of finance and -5.9 percent as net source of finance.

3. Industrial enterprises. Other accounts payable are included in loans, not in short-term securities and payables.

Source: OECD Financial Statistics III: Non-Financial Enterprises Financial Statements, 1990 and 1992.

As both gross and net source of finance, loans were, as expected, most important for Japanese firms and least important for American firms with Swedish and French firms in between. For Swedish and French firms, the sum of retentions, short-term securities and payables, and loans, as net sources of finance, exceeded non-financial investment, while shares and bonds were negative net sources.

This indicates that Swedish and French firms used loans to fund their activities as institutional investors to a greater extent than Japanese and American firms. Such an activity may increase knowledge diffusion between firms, thus improving the efficiency of the use of knowledge in the innovation process, but may as well divert funds into unrelated activities.

Evidence from the USA suggests that M&A has limited rewards and decreases intangible investments, such as R&D (Porter, 1992, and OECD, 1995). In this context, an interesting research topic would be to study whether M&A has the same effect on economies with strong bank-industry networks.

Table 5.8 shows that the ratio of financial investment to non-financial investment is low in both Japan and the USA compared to France and above all Sweden.

The overborrowing of Swedish industrial firms considering that their financing needs for non-financial investment may be covered by retentions, indicates that Swedish industrial firms are heavily involved in banking and finance, so that industrial banking has been internalized by the firms. The Swedish ratio was very high, suggesting that network links were sustained by industrial firms acting as financial holdings. Such a development would be natural, since collective action had imposed upper bounds on the bank convention in Sweden.

Table 5.8 Ratio of Financial Investment to Non-Financial Investment of Non-Financial Corporations

	Japan[1]	Sweden	France[2]	USA
1982	0.32	1.22	0.56	0.17
1983	0.53	1.27	1.01	0.40
1984	0.87	1.22	0.85	0.26
1985	0.46	1.00	0.52	0.22
1986	0.78	1.77	1.24	0.43
1987	0.83	1.82	1.15	0.30
1988	0.91	1.80	1.52	0.40
1989	0.99	1.74	1.60	0.26
1990	0.56	1.53	1.01	0.22

Notes:
1. Total sample.
2. Industrial firms.

Source: OECD Financial Statistics III: Non-Financial Enterprises Financial Statements, 1990 and 1992.

According to Table 5.9, Swedish industrial firms have used an increasing share of their large financial investments for financing of their affiliates[3] either by loans or by investment in new equity shares.

Table 5.9 Swedish Non-Financial Corporations' Financing[1] of Affiliates as Share of Their Financial Investment (in percent)

1982	1983	1984	1985	1986	1987	1988	1989	1990
22.2	34.4	48.8	61.4	54.8	67.4	69.6	75.5	89.3

Note:
1. Financing by loans, including short-term trade credits to affiliates, and increase in equity shareholding.

Source: OECD Financial Statistics III: Non-Financial Enterprises Financial Statements, 1992.

This indicates that the bank convention in Sweden was sustained by internalized industrial banking in Sweden. Loans had a positive net contribution to non-financial investment, although retentions would have been sufficient. Learning-by-financing took place within the internal banks of industrial firms as well as in the banks.

In France, the bank convention had been supported by collective action, but during the 1980s support by collective action was beneficial to the bond convention. The government had during the 1980s encouraged the expansion of capital markets (Patat, 1987, Bisignano, 1992). For French firms, bank loans were less important than shares as gross source of finance. French banks have, as institutional investors, built up strong links with industry as well as insurance companies (Pastré, 1992).

French firms have, however, not internalized industrial banking, like Swedish firms, but have become institutional investors. This may be seen in Table 5.10 which gives trade investments (participations) in percent of financial investment.

Table 5.10 French Industrial Enterprises' Trade Investments as Share of Their Financial Investment (in percent)

1982	1983	1984	1985	1986	1987	1988	1989	1990
16.6	14.5	21.8	31.0	51.5	58.5	56.7	55.2	78.9

Source: OECD Financial Statistics III: Non-Financial Enterprises Financial Statements, 1992.

As the links to affiliates are closer than to firms where one makes trade investments, this suggests lower internal learning-by-financing than between firms of Swedish industrial groups. In Sweden, the banks have more competition in industrial banking from industry itself.

Summing up, a comparison of liquidity, solvency, and the financing of industry shows that in Japan where the bank convention remained dominant, loans were very important as financing source compared to retentions, and in the USA where the bond convention remained dominant, loans did hardly matter.

As the securitized economy evolved, the institutional endowment of network commitment was challenged, but the bank convention remained viable in France, although somewhat weaker due to collective action, while the Swedish bank convention was viable with industrial firms as bankers. In hybrid financial systems with industrial firms as institutional investors, both Sweden and France, nevertheless, maintained a viable bank convention in between the bank convention-dominated Japan and the bond convention-dominated USA. This coexistence of financial systems suggests that bank-industry networks around universal banks remained viable, like the networks around venture capitalists.

5.4 Network Commitment and Trust versus Control as Creditors' Approach

The principal-agent story is one where bankers and market investors must find a way to control the entrepreneurs. The more financing they supply, the more they have to control the entrepreneurs. Mayer and Alexander (1990) argue that the market for corporate control and bank control over firms explain differences between Germany and the UK. Bank-industry networks are, however, based on network commitment and mutual trust between informed bankers and reliable entrepreneurs, something which does not exist between an arm's length market investor and an entrepreneur. This is the moral foundation behind learning-by-financing which, according to my theoretical analysis, decreases the information costs of the banker and thereby the credit costs of the entrepreneur. In the real world, this should be reflected in the higher relative importance of loans to retentions as financing source.

Debt finance seems correlated with short-term liabilities and the propensity to financing by bank loans with short-term loans (OECD, 1995). The casual interpretation maintains, however, that short-term loans expresses a lack of trust in the firms, but why would debt finance be more common if the creditors' trust is smaller? Rivaud-Danset and Salais (1992) point out how short-term debt increases liquidity and thereby the freedom of action of the Japanese firms. This connection between the high ratio of short-term debt on the liability side and the high ratio of cash and deposits at the asset side was noted already by Aoki (1988). When short-term debt increases liquidity and thereby the freedom of action of the firms, creditors express their commitment to and trust in these firms.[4] The increase in R&D costs and the shortening of the product cycle give cash requirement peaks during the innovation process, but periodic surges in borrowing requirements can be met by short-term lending from informed financial institutions (OECD, 1995).

In their comparison between the financing of German and UK firms, Mayer and Alexander (1990) argues that the high proportion of long-term debt of German firms was an expression of a tighter control by German banks, because long-term debt is expected to be associated with tighter control of creditors over debtors, otherwise the latter could divert cash resources. Hence, if the proportion of long-term credit increases, then the control of creditors over debtors become tighter. A high proportion of short-term debt would, therefore, be associated with a less control-oriented approach of creditors towards their debtors. This is what happens when creditors through their short-term credits increase the liquidity of industrial firms. By giving industrial firms more freedom of action, they express commitment to and trust in these firms.

In this context, one should bear in mind the differences in commitment between the bank convention and the bond convention. Using Hirschman's (1970) terminology, a high share of short-term debt would be associated with creditors having bond convention exit rights or bank convention voice rights. Exit and voice should not be put together as liquidation rights. Voice rights involve a commitment of creditors to the debtors, something exit rights do not. According to Berglöf (1990), banks take over the control rights through bank-led reorganizations in bank-oriented systems only in bad states of nature, while the hostile takeovers of market-oriented systems give the market the control rights through hostile takeovers in both good and bad states of nature. Hence, bank-oriented systems allow firms more freedom of action.

When the bank convention is strong with loans being important compared to retentions as financing source, a high proportion of short-term debt would indicate that the creditors have trust in their client firms, that is the bank-industry networks are strong and viable. In other words, they are willing to contribute to the liquidity of industrial firms through short-term credit.

Table 5.11 shows the ratio of short-term liabilities to long-term liabilities, i.e. the ratio of short-term debt to long-term debt, on the balance sheet of industrial firms, excluding trade credits. French and Japanese firms had a very high proportion of short-term debt, Swedish firms a slightly lower one, although the Japanese declining ratio and the Swedish improving one made the Swedish ratio higher than the Japanese one in 1989 and 1990.

Even the French ratio of short-term debt to long-term debt had a temporary decline during the mid 1980s. The most striking result, however, is the very low and declining proportion of short-term debt of American firms. A declining ratio means that short-term loans are relatively unimportant as financing source compared to long-term loans and vice versa for an improving ratio.

The long-term nature of American corporate debt indicates creditors having control over debtors, because American firms had a lower liquidity (see Table 5.5), while the more bank convention dominated systems had creditors who showed more trust in the debtors. After all, the informed network bankers (bank convention) may trust their industrial clients to an extent that arm's length bankers (bond convention) cannot. The lack of historically evolved mutual trust between bankers and entrepreneurs of the bond convention calls for some contractual control mechanism.

Table 5.11 Ratio of Short-Term Liabilities to Long-Term Liabilities, excluding Trade Credits, of Non-Financial Corporations

	Japan[1]	France[2]	Sweden	USA
1982	1.58	1.64	0.88	0.43
1983	1.57	1.67	0.89	0.41
1984	1.58	1.47	0.97	0.43
1985	1.52	1.44	1.05	0.39
1986	1.51	1.38	1.12	0.35
1987	1.39	1.50	1.26	0.30
1988	1.37	1.43	1.29	0.28
1989	1.21	1.76	1.47	0.26
1990	1.16	1.68	1.55	0.23

Notes:
1. Total sample.
2. Industrial firms.

Source: OECD Financial Statistics III: Non-Financial Enterprises Financial Statements, 1990 and 1992.

In Germany where the firms have a high proportion of long-term debt, according to Mayer and Alexander (1990), the lack of financial markets - not the universal banks and their industrial groups - seems to be the reason behind financial stability (Kregel, 1992, and Aglietta and Moutot, 1993). In contrast, Japan, France, and Sweden have developed financial markets as well as bank-industry networks.

If bankers trust their industrial clients, then market investors may still try to control the industrial enterprises, thus reducing the freedom of action of entrepreneurs. High dividends may be a response to market control, as argued by Mayer and Alexander (1990), but the larger the dividends' share of cash flow, the smaller the retentions become. The freedom of action of industrial firms might, therefore, be assessed by studying the ratio of retentions to gross trading profit, shown in Table 5.12. Gross trading profit is defined as value added minus wages and social charges. The higher the ratio of retentions to gross trading profit, the more autonomous the firms are.

The lower the solvency for each level of freedom action of industrial firms, the greater the creditors' trust is, since they are willing to extend credit without decreasing the freedom of action of the firms. The freedom of action of industrial firms converged for the four countries in 1990. In 1982, Swedish firms had a very high freedom of action and French firms a very low one due to their overborrowing.

The Japanese freedom of action of industrial firms was initially lower than the American one, but increased during the 1982-85 period. The freedom of action of Swedish firms dropped between 1988 and 1990, something which coincided with a decline in solvency (see Table 5.6) after the Swedish financial system had been deregulated and the bond convention had gained ground. Similarly, the greater freedom of action of Japanese firms and above all French firms coincided with higher solvency. Creditors' trust seems to have allowed a lower solvency in Japan than in the USA with Sweden and France in between, something being reflected in the differences in the importance of loans as net source of finance (see Table 5.7).

The solvency creditors may tolerate is, however, dependent on the rationalization pressure. According to Schön (1994), the rationalization pressure follows cyclical patterns and culminates when there are wage peaks in relation to value added.

Table 5.12 Ratio of Retentions to Gross Trading Profit of Non-Financial Corporations

	Japan[1]	France[2]	Sweden	USA
1982	0.46	0.33	0.74	0.59
1983	0.50	0.38	0.74	0.61
1984	0.51	0.47	0.71	0.61
1985	0.56	0.44	0.69	0.62
1986	0.56	0.50	0.67	0.59
1987	0.57	0.47	0.67	0.60
1988	0.59	0.51	0.70	0.59
1989	0.58	0.59	0.61	0.56
1990	0.56	0.58	0.57	0.57

Notes:
1. Total sample.
2. Industrial firms.

Source: OECD Financial Statistics III: Non-Financial Enterprises Financial Statements, 1990 and 1992.

Table 5.13 Ratio of Wages to Value Added of Non-Financial Corporations

	Japan[1]	France[2]	Sweden	USA
1982	0.72	0.73	0.75	0.74
1983	0.71	0.73	0.71	0.73
1984	0.70	0.72	0.71	0.72
1985	0.69	0.73	0.72	0.73
1986	0.71	0.72	0.73	0.74
1987	0.68	0.69	0.72	0.73
1988	0.67	0.64	0.71	0.73
1989	0.67	0.62	0.72	0.73
1990	0.66	0.64	0.74	0.74

Notes:
1. Total sample.
2. Industrial firms.

Source: OECD Financial Statistics III: Non-Financial Enterprises Financial Statements, 1990 and 1992.

Table 5.13 shows the ratio of wages to value added, as a measure of the rationalization pressure. The convergence of the freedom of action of industrial firms in 1990 have required a divergence of rationalization pressure. The same freedom of action of industrial firms requires a lower rationalization pressure in France and Japan. This suggests a lower tolerance limit among creditors and owners before discipline had to be imposed, thus indicating a somewhat lower level of creditors' trust, given the level of solvency.

The very low solvency and the great importance of loans as source of finance of Japanese firms explain why Japanese creditors and owners were less willing to tolerate a high rationalization pressure, but French firms enjoyed a smaller creditors' trust. This is consistent with Fukuyama's (1995) view of France as a low-trust society. Yet, French firms were allowed to use loans as source of finance to a greater extent than American firms and to keep a lower solvency. Creditors' trust in the USA requires a high solvency due to the strength of the bond convention.

Summing up, both the ratio of short-term debt to long-term debt and the ratio of retentions to gross profits suggest that the lower solvency and the greater relative importance of loans compared to retentions as financing source for non-financial investment of Japanese, French, and Swedish firms are based on creditors' having more trust in their industrial client firms. Network commitment between bankers and entrepreneurs, the foundation for a bank-industry network, was high. In other words, this indicates a relative strong bank convention, yielding a high liquidity in industry. Network commitment remained stable during the 1982-90 period.

5.5 Summary

My purpose in this chapter was to analyze the evolutionary viability of the bank convention in a securitized economy by making an assessment of industrial finance conventions according to their liquidity and solvency. Referring to the evolutionary Stag Hunt game, this chapter studies whether the payoff structure has changed with the evolution of the securitized economy. How has Swedish and French industrial finance systems developed in relation the Japanese and American ones during the 1982-90 period? Was the bank convention still viable?

A comparison of debt/equity ratios and bank loans' share of total liabilities suggests that the industrial finance systems of Japan, France, Sweden, and the USA differ, the banks remaining most important in Japan and least important in the USA with France and Sweden in between. Macroeconomic indicators of financial development, the ratio of broad money to GDP (M2/GDP) and the ratio of claims of the banking system on the non-financial sector to GDP, suggest a much lower importance of commercial banks in the Swedish economy.

In the analysis of liquidity, solvency, and industrial finance conventions, the bank convention is associated with a higher liquidity and lower solvency than the bond convention. The bank convention had its stronghold in Japan (high liquidity, low solvency) and the bond convention in the USA (low liquidity, high solvency). The hybrid industrial finance systems in France and Sweden (medium liquidity, medium solvency) positioned themselves in between. This was reflected in the relative importance of loans as source of finance. As net financing source, loans were very important in Japan, while they hardly mattered the USA. Again, Sweden and France positioned themselves in between.

As the securitized economy evolved, the institutional endowment of network commitment was challenged, but the bank convention remained viable in France, although somewhat weaker due to collective action supporting the bond convention, while the Swedish bank convention was viable with industrial firms as bankers. Hence, in hybrid financial systems with industrial firms as institutional investors, reflected in high ratios of financial to non-financial investments, Sweden and France maintained a viable bank convention in between the bank convention-dominated Japan and the bond convention-dominated USA. This coexistence of financial systems suggests that bank-industry networks around universal banks remained viable, like the networks around venture capitalists.

In Sweden financial investments were very important, suggesting that network links were sustained by industrial firms acting as financial holdings. Such a development would be natural, since collective action had imposed upper bounds on the bank convention in Sweden. In France, the bank convention had been supported by collective action, but during the 1980s support by collective action was beneficial to the bond convention.

Yet, one must remember that network commitment and trust between bankers and entrepreneurs is the foundation for bank-industry networks and the viability of the bank convention. The higher ratio of short-term debt to long-term debt together with the higher liquidity of Japanese, French, and

Swedish firms indicate that their creditors had more trust in them than the creditors of American firms. Their higher ratio of short-term debt to long-term debt reflected network commitment and trust rather than control.

The ratio of retentions to gross profits indicates convergence in the freedom of action of industrial firms in 1990, although there were differences in solvency and in the importance of loans as source of finance. This suggests more mutual trust between bankers and entrepreneurs for Japanese, French, and Swedish firms and their respective creditors, as compared to American firms. Creditors' trust required a lower rationalization pressure in Japan and France in order to allow for a high level of debt finance. Nevertheless, the bank-industry network approach explains the viability of the bank convention in Sweden and France, because freedom of action of industrial firms is combined with more debt finance. Network commitment remained stable during the 1982-90 period.

Notes

1. See e.g. Barro (1991) and Mankiw, Romer and Weil (1992).

2. Net sources refer to the net contribution of a particular financing source towards non-financial investment.

3. Affiliates are defined as parent companies, subsidiaries, and "sister" corporations having the same parent company.

4. Short-term lending in bad states of nature to non-innovative firms is an exception that could reflect a lack of trust.

6 Schumpeterian Banker-Entrepreneur Interaction, Learning-by-Financing, and Bank-Industry Networks: A General Conclusion

The topic of this book has been Schumpeterian banker-entrepreneur interaction and bank-industry networks. My purpose was to give an answer to three questions:

(i) How does learning-by-financing within bank-industry networks influence the quality upgrading of the economic process?

(ii) How do bank-industry networks evolve through evolutionary selection as bankers and entrepreneurs interact?

(iii) What conditions are crucial for the evolutionary viability of the universal bank as network bank in a securitized economy?

The view that the bank-industry network around a universal bank is viable as institutional form for industrial banking in a securitized economy has received theoretical foundations.

The general argument for the view above was developed in chapter 2. Learning-by-financing within a bank-industry network allows for financial stability as well as industrial experimentation. Universal banking integrates allocation-by-exploration with allocation-by-selection by relying on the voice mechanism rather than the exit mechanism of securities markets. Learning-by-financing has a positive role to play also in the securitized economy and provides the condition for bank-industry networks around universal banks. In other words, the value of information is higher than the value of diversification also in the securitized economy.

How systemic differences in learning-by-financing influence growth regimes and quality upgrading of the economic process was analyzed in chapter 3. Financial institutions were added to the Grossman-Helpman endogenous growth model with quality ladders, enlarging and enriching the model with institutional differences in Schumpeterian banker-entrepreneur interaction and the consequences of bank-industry networks for growth regimes. Strong bank-industry networks imply a high learning-by-financing which in turn increases innovativeness, since the resource allocation improves when the banker is informed.

Institutional change and the evolution of bank-industry networks were considered in chapter 4. Schumpeterian banker-entrepreneur interaction was analyzed as an evolutionary Stag Hunt game to provide a functionalist-evolutionary explanation why bank-industry networks exist in a world with uncertainty and bounded rationality. The evolutionary Stag Hunt game gives two evolutionary stable strategies: (i) the bank convention with bankers and entrepreneurs cooperating within bank-industry networks and (ii) the bond convention with independent bankers and entrepreneurs.

The bank convention may evolve spontaneously only when institutional endowments, such as developed banking and network commitment, are sufficient. Otherwise, collective action to design privileged groups is necessary.

A historical analysis indicates that the banking system and the network commitment were sufficient institutional endowments in Sweden, thus making the bank convention viable. In France, however, banking and network commitment were insufficient as institutional endowments, so the bank convention was not viable.

The French bank-industry networks evolved through collective action by the French government, making the bank convention fully privileged, while Swedish collective action was aimed at putting upper bounds on the bank convention, but tended to do so on the bond convention as well.

The viability analysis was continued in chapter 5 with an assessment about the viability of the bank convention in the evolving securitized economy. Sweden and France were compared to Japan as the stronghold of the bank convention and the USA as the stronghold of the bond convention.

As the securitized economy evolved, the institutional endowment of network commitment was challenged, but the bank convention seemed viable in France, although somewhat weaker due to collective action supporting the bond convention, while the Swedish bank convention was viable with industrial firms as bankers. Industrial firms functioned as institutional investors in the hybrid financial systems of Sweden and France in between Japan and the USA. This coexistence of financial systems suggests that bank-industry networks around universal banks remained viable, like the networks around venture capitalists.

A study of liquidity, solvency, and sources of finance suggests that learning-by-financing maintained a function within the emerging securitized economy, thus keeping the bank convention evolutionary viable. The value of information seems to have remained higher than the value of diversification when network commitment was present.

Finally, we have arrived at the concluding remarks. Learning-by-financing within bank-industry networks may increase innovativeness and thereby the quality upgrading of the economic process through a better resource allocation at lower information costs. Bank-industry networks may evolve spontaneously through a history of successful interaction between bankers and entrepreneurs when network commitment is a sufficient institutional endowment, otherwise collective action, where the government designs privileged groups, is required. Bank-industry networks around universal banks are evolutionary viable in a securitized economy, provided that learning-by-financing and network commitment keep the value of information higher than the value of diversification.

References

Adam, M.C., and A. Farber, (1988), "Le financement de l'innovation téchnologique. Deuxième partie: L'apport de la théorie financière", *Cahiers Economique de Bruxelles*, No.117, 1st quarter.

Aghion, Philippe, and Peter Howitt, (1992), "A Model of Growth through Creative Destruction", *Econometrica*, 60, 323-351.

Aglietta, Michel, Anton Brender and Virginie Coudert, (1990), *Globalisation financière: L'aventure obligée*, Paris: Economica.

Aglietta, Michel, and Philippe Moutot, (1993), "L'évolution des structures financières des grands pays et la prévention du risque de système dans l'union économique et monétaire", *Banque de France. Cahiers économique et monétaire*, No.41, 55-81.

Amendola, Mario, and Jean-Luc Gaffard, (1988), *La dynamique économique de l'innovation*, Paris: Economica.

Andersen, Esben S., (1991), "Techno-Economic Paradigms as Typical Interfaces between Producers and Users", *Journal of Evolutionary Economics*, 1, 119-144.

Aoki, Masahiko, (1988), *Information, Incentives, and Bargaining in the Japanese Economy*, Cambridge: Cambridge University Press.

Aoki, Masahiko, Hugh Patrick, and Paul Sheard, (1994), "The Japanese Main Bank System: An Introductory Overview", in Masahiko Aoki and Hugh Patrick (eds.), *The Japanese Main Bank System: Its Relevance for Developing and Transforming Economies*, Oxford: Oxford University Press.

Arrow, Kenneth J., (1962), "The Economic Implications of Learning by Doing", *Review of Economic Studies*, 29, 155-173.

Arthur, W. Brian, (1988), " Competing Technologies: An Overview", in Dosi, Giovanni, Christopher Freeman, Richard Nelson, Gerald Silverberg, and Luc Soete (eds.), *Technical Change and Economic Theory*, London: Pinter Publishers.

Artus, Patrick, (1990), *Crise des intermédiaires americains. Le marché sait-il compte du risque?*, Caisse des Dépots et Consignations, Working Paper 1190-23/E.

Axelrod, Robert, (1984), *The Evolution of Cooperation*, New York: Basic Books.

Ballot, Gérard, and Erol Taymaz, (1998), "Human Capital, Technological Lock-in, and Evolutionary Dynamics", in Gunnar Eliasson and Christopher Green (eds.), *Microfoundations of Economic Growth: A Schumpeterian Perspective*, Ann Arbor, MI: University of Michigan Press.

Barro, Robert J., (1991), "Economic Growth in a Cross Section of Countries, *Quarterly Journal of Economics*, 105, 407-437.

Becchetti, Leonardo, (1995), "Finance, Investment, and Innovation: A Theoretical and Empirical Analysis", *Empirica*, 22, 167-184.

Becker, Gary S., (1992), "Habits, Addictions, and Transitions", *Kyklos*, 45, 327-346.

Beduc, L., F. Ducruzet, and P. Papadacci, (1992), "The French Financial System", in George G. Kaufman (ed.), *Banking Structures in Major Countries*, Boston/Dordrecht/London: Kluwer.

Bellon, Bertrand, (1980), *Le pouvoir financier et l'industrie en France*, Paris: Editions du Seuil.

Berglöf, Erik, (1988), *Ägarna och kontrollen över företaget - en jämförande studie av sex länders finansiella system*, SOU 1988:38, Ägande och inflytande i svenskt näringsliv, Bilaga 12, Stockholm: Ministry of Industry.

Berglöf, Erik, (1990), *Corporate Control and Capital Structure: Essays on Property Rights and Financial Contracts*, Dissertation, Stockholm School of Economics.

Berglöf, Erik, and Hans Sjögren (1995), "Husbanksrelationen i omvandling - förbindelserna mellan affärsbanker och storföretag i svenskt näringsliv 1985-1993", in *Bankerna under krisen: Fyra rapporter till Bankkriskommittén*, Stockholm: Ministry of Finance.

Bernanke, Ben, and Mark Gertler, (1990), "Financial Fragility and Economic Performance", *Quarterly Journal of Economics*, 105, 87-114.

Bisignano, Joseph, (1992), "Banking in the European Community: Structure, Competition, and Public Policy", in George G. Kaufman (ed.), *Banking Structures in Major Countries*, Boston/Dordrecht/London: Kluwer.

Bjuggren, Per-Olof, (1985), *A Transaction Cost Approach to Vertical Integration: The Case of the Swedish Pulp and Paper Industry*, Lund: Lund Economic Studies.

Bonin, Hubert, (1987), *Suez du canal à la finance (1858-1987)*, Paris: Economica.

Boyer, Robert, (1986), *La théorie de la régulation: Une analyse critique*, Paris: La Découverte.

Campbell, Tim S., and William A. Kracaw, (1980), "Information Production, Market Signalling, and the Theory of Financial Information, *Journal of Finance*, 35, 863-882.

Chang, Ha-Joon, and Richard Kozul-Wright, (1994), "Organising Development: Comparing the National Systems of Entrepreneurship in Sweden and South Korea", *Journal of Development Studies*, 30, 859-891.

Coleman, James S., (1988), "Social Capital in the Creation of Human Capital", *American Journal of Sociology*, 94 Suppl, S95-S120.

Dahmén, Erik, (1950), *Svensk industriell företagarverksamhet: Kausalanalys av den industriella utvecklingen 1919-1939 (English summary: Entrepreneurial Activity in Swedish Industry in the Period 1919-1939)*, Stockholm: IUI.

Dahmén, Erik, (1988), "'Development Blocks' in Industrial Economics", *Scandinavian Economic History Review*, 36, 3-14.

David, Paul, (1985), "Clio and the Economics of QWERTY", *American Economic Review*, 75, 332-337.

Davidson, Paul, (1978), *Money and the Real World*, 2nd ed, London: Macmillan.

Davies, Glyn, (1994), *A History of Money: From Ancient Times to the Present Day*, Cardiff: University of Wales Press.

Day, Richard H., Gunnar Eliasson, and Clas Wihlborg, (1993), "Markets for Innovation, Ownership, and Control: Toward a Synthesis", in Richard H. Day, Gunnar Eliasson, and Clas Wihlborg (eds.), *The Markets for Innovation, Ownership, and Control*, Amsterdam/London/New York/Tokyo: North-Holland.

de Meza, David, and David C. Webb, (1987), "Too Much Investment: A Problem of Asymmetric Information", *Quarterly Journal of Economics*, 102, 281-292.

Desai, Meghnad, and William Low, (1987), "Measuring the Opportunity for Product Innovation", in Marcello De Cecco (ed.), *Changing Money: Financial Innovation in Developed Countries*, Oxford: Basil Blackwell.

Diamond, Douglas W, (1984), "Financial Intermediation and Delegated Monitoring", *Review of Economic Studies*, 51, 393-414.

Dosi, Giovanni, (1984), *Technical Change and Industrial Transformation: The Theory and an Application to the Semiconductor Industry*, London: Macmillan.

Dosi, Giovanni, (1990), "Finance, Innovation and Industrial Change", *Journal of Economic Behavior and Organization*, 13, 299-319.

Eliasson, Gunnar, (1985), *The Firm and Financial Markets in the Swedish Micro-to-Macro Model: Theory, Model, and Verification*, Stockholm: IUI.

Eliasson, Gunnar, (1990), "The Firm as a Competent Team", *Journal of Economic Behavior and Organization*, 13, 275-298.

Eliasson, Gunnar, (1992), "Business Competence, Organizational Learning, and Economic Growth: Establishing the Smith-Schumpeter-Wicksell (SSW) Connection", in Frederic M. Scherer and Mark Perlman (eds.), *Innovation and Economic Growth: Studies in the Schumpeterian Tradition*, Ann Arbor, MI: University of Michigan Press.

Eliasson, Gunnar, (1996), "Spillovers, Integrated Production, and the Theory of the Firm, *Journal of Evolutionary Economics*, 6, 125-140.

Elster, Jon, (1979), *Ulysses and the Sirens: Studies in Rationality and Irrationality*, Cambridge: Cambridge University Press.

Engwall, Lars, and Jan Johanson, (1989), *Banks in Industrial Networks*, Department of Business Studies, Uppsala University, Working Paper No. 1989/2.

Ergas, Henry, (1985), *Why Do Some Countries Innovate More than Others*, CEPS Papers No.5, Brussels.

Etzioni, Amitai, (1988), *The Moral Dimension: Toward a New Economics*, New York: Free Press.

Fama, Eugene, (1985), "What's Different about Banks?", *Journal of Monetary Economics*, 15, 29-39.

Frank, Robert H., (1988), *Passion within Reason: The Strategic Role of the Emotions*, New York: Norton.

Freedeman, Charles E., (1993), *The Triumph of Corporate Capitalism in France 1867-1914,* Rochester: University of Rochester Press.

Friedman, Daniel, (1991), "Evolutionary Games in Economics", *Econometrica*, 59, 637-666.

Fukuyama, Francis, (1995), *Trust: The Social Virtues and the Creation of Prosperity*, London: Hamish Hamilton.

Georgescu-Roegen, Nicholas, (1971), *The Entropy Law and the Economic Process*, Cambridge, MA: Harvard University Press.

Gerlach, Michael L., (1992), *Alliance Capitalism: The Social Organization of Japanese Business*, Berkley: University of California Press.

Gertler, Mark, R. Glenn Hubbard, and Anil Kashyap, (1991), "Interest Rate Spreads, Credit Constraints, and Investment Fluctuations: An Empirical Investigation", in R. Glenn Hubbard (ed.), *Financial Markets and Financial Crises*, Chicago: University of Chicago Press.

Glete, Jan, (1994), *Nätverk i näringslivet: Ägande och industriell omvandling i det mogna industrisamhället 1920-1990*, Stockholm: SNS Förlag.

Glete, Jan, (1998), "Entrepreneurs and Social Elites: Some Reflections on the Case of Sweden", in Gunnar Eliasson and Christopher Green (eds.), *Microfoundations of Economic Growth: A Schumpeterian Perspective*, Ann Arbor, MI: University of Michigan Press.

Goldberg, Michael A., (1994), "Trading Local Autonomy for Economic Efficiency or the Faustian Bargain of Choice at the Close of the Twentieth Century: The Case of Globalized Financial and Property Markets", in Börje Johansson, Charlie Karlsson, and Lars Westin (eds.), *Patterns of a Network Economy*, Berlin/Heidelberg: Springer-Verlag.

Granovetter, Mark, (1985), "Economic Action and Social Structure: The Problem of Embeddedness", *American Journal of Sociology*, 91, 481-510.

Granovetter, Mark, (1995), "Coase Revisited: Business Groups in the Modern Economy", *Industrial and Corporate Change*, 4, 93-130.

Green, Diana, (1986), "The State, Finance, and Industry in France", in Andrew Cox (ed.), *State, Finance, and Industry: A Comparative Analysis of Post-War Trends in Six Advanced Industrial Economies*, Brighton: Wheatsheaf Books.

Grimmett, Geoffrey, and David Stirzaker, (1982), *Probability and Random Processes*, Oxford: Clarendon Press.

Grossman, Gene M. and Elhanan Helpman, (1991a), *Innovation and Growth in the Global Economy*, Cambridge, MA: MIT Press.

Grossman, Gene M. and Elhanan Helpman, (1991b), "Quality Ladders in the Theory of Growth", *Review of Economic Studies*, 58, 43-61.

Gueslin, André, (1992), "Banks and State in France from the 1880s to the 1930s: The Impossible Advance of the Banks", in Youssef Cassis (ed.), *Finance and Financiers in European History, 1880-1960*, Cambridge: Cambridge University Press.

Gurley, John G., and E.S. Shaw, (1955), "Financial Aspects of Economic Development", *American Economic Review*, 45, 515-538.

Gönenç, Rauf, (1988), "La signification industrielle de la mutation financière", *Revue d'Economie Financière*, No. 5-6, 67-84.

Gönenç, Rauf, (1991), "Les trois formes de gestion financière des risques industriels", *Revue d'Economie Financière*, No. 18, 131-146.

Heiner, Ronald A., (1988a), "Imperfect Decisions and Routinized Production: Implications for Evolutionary Modeling and Inertial Technical Change", in Dosi, Giovanni, Christopher Freeman, Richard Nelson, Gerald Silverberg, and Luc Soete (eds.), *Technical Change and Economic Theory*, London: Pinter Publishers.

Heiner, Ronald A., (1988b), "Imperfect Decisions in Organizations: Toward a Theory of Internal Structure", *Journal of Economic Behavior and Organization*, 9, 25-44.

Hildebrand, Karl-Gustaf, (1971), *I omvandlingens tjänst: Svenska Handelsbanken 1871-1955*, Stockholm: Esselte.

Hildebrand, Karl-Gustaf, (1985), *Expansion Crisis Reconstruction 1917-1939*, Stockholm: Liber Förlag.

Hirschman, Albert, (1970), *Exit, Voice, and Loyalty: Responses to Decline in Firms, Organizations, and States*, Cambridge, MA: Harvard University Press.

Hodgson, Geoffrey M., (1989), "Post-Keynesianism and Institutionalism: The Missing Link", in John Pheby (ed.), *New Directions in Post-Keynesian Economics*, Aldershot: Edward Elgar.

Hoshi, Takeo, Anil Kashyap, and David Scharfstein, (1991), "Corporate Structure, Liquidity, and Investment: Evidence from Japanese Industrial Groups", *Quarterly Journal of Economics*, 106, 33-60.

Håkansson, Håkan, (1989), *Corporate Technological Behavior: Co-operation and Networks*, London: Routledge.

Iwai, Katsuhito, (1984a), "Schumpeterian Dynamics: An Evolutionary Model of Innovation and Imitation", *Journal of Economic Behavior and Organization*, 5, 159-190.

Iwai, Katsuhito, (1984b), "Schumpeterian Dynamics II: Technological Progress, Firm Growth and Economic Selection", *Journal of Economic Behavior and Organization*, 5, 321-351.

James, Christopher, (1987), "Some Evidence on the Uniqueness of Bank Loans", *Journal of Financial Economics*, 19, 217-235.

Johansson, Börje, and Lars Westin, (1994), "Revealing Network Properties of Sweden's Trade with Europe", in Börje Johansson, Charlie Karlsson, and Lars Westin (eds.), *Patterns of a Network Economy*, Berlin/Heidelberg: Springer-Verlag.

Kahneman, Daniel, Jack Knetch, and Richard Thaler, (1990), "Experimental Tests of the Endowment Effect and the Coase Theorem", *Journal of Political Economy*, 98, 1325-1348.

Karlsson, Charlie, and Lars Westin, (1994), "Patterns of a Network Economy - An Introduction", in Börje Johansson, Charlie Karlsson, and Lars Westin (eds.), *Patterns of a Network Economy*, Berlin/Heidelberg: Springer-Verlag.

Kindleberger, Charles P., (1984), *A Financial History of Western Europe*, London: George Allen & Unwin.

King, Robert G., and Ross Levine, (1993), *Finance and Growth: Schumpeter Might Be Right*, World Bank Policy Research Working Paper, WPS 1083, Washington, DC.

Kirzner, Israel, (1973), *Competition and Entrepreneurship*, Chicago: University of Chicago Press.

Klein, Burton, (1977), *Dynamic Economics*, Cambridge, MA: Harvard University Press.

Knight, Frank, (1921), *Risk, Uncertainty, and Profit*, Boston: Houghton Mifflin.

Kregel, Jan A., (1992), "Institutional Investors and Financial Markets in Britain, the USA and Germany", Paper prepared for the working conference on Financial Institutions and Regulatory Regimes in Europe from the 1930s to the 1990s, Harvard University, January 14-15, 1993.

Kurgan-van Hentenryk, G., (1992), "Finance and Financiers in Belgium, 1880-1940", in Youssef Cassis (ed.), *Finance and Financiers in European History, 1880-1960*, Cambridge: Cambridge University Press.

Langlois, Richard N., (1986), "Rationality, Institutions, and Explanation", in Richard N. Langlois (ed.), *Economics as a Process: Essays in the New Institutional Economics*, New York: Cambridge University Press.

Langlois, Richard N., and Paul L. Robertson, (1995), *Firms, Markets and Economic Change: A Dynamic Theory of Business Institutions*, London/New York: Routledge.

Larsson, Mats, (1995), "Overcoming Institutional Barriers: Financial Networks in Sweden 1910-90", in Youssef Cassis, Gerald D. Feldman, and Ulf Olsson (eds.), *The Evolution of Financial Institutions and Markets in Twentieth-*

Century Europe, Aldershot: Edward Elgar.

Larsson, Mats, and Håkan Lindgren, (1992), "The Political Economy of Banking: Retail Banking and Corporate Finance in Sweden, 1850-1939", in Youssef Cassis (ed.), *Finance and Financiers in European History, 1880-1960*, Cambridge: Cambridge University Press.

Lindgren, Håkan, (1990), "Long-Term Contracts in Financial Markets: Bank-Industry Connections in Sweden, Illustrated by the Operations of Stockholms Enskilda Bank 1900-70", in Masahiko Aoki, Bo Gustafsson, and Oliver E. Williamson (eds.), *The Firm as a Nexus of Treaties*, London: Sage.

Lindgren, Håkan, (1994), *Aktivt ägande: Investor under växlande konjunkturer*, Stockholm: EHF.

Lundberg, Erik, (1961), *Produktivitet och räntabilitet: Studier i kapitalets betydelse inom svenskt näringsliv*, Stockholm: SNS.

Lundström, Ragnhild, (1994), "Continuity and Change in Swedish Banking", in Alice Teichova, Terry Gourvich, and Agnes Pogány (eds.), *Universal Banking in the Twentieth Century: Finance, Industry, and the State in North and Central Europe*, Aldershot: Edward Elgar.

Lundvall, Bengt-Åke, (1991), "Explaining Inter-Firm Cooperation and Innovation: Limits of the Transaction Cost Approach", mimeo, Institute for Production, Aalborg University, March.

MacKie-Mason, Jeffrey K., (1989), *Do Firms Care Who Provides their Financing?*, NBER Working Paper No.3039, Cambridge, MA.

Mankiw, Gregory N., David Romer, and David N. Neal, (1992), "A Contribution to the Empirics of Economic Growth", *Quarterly Journal of Economics*, 107, 408-437.

Marmefelt, Thomas, (1997), "Network Commitment as Institutional Endowment and the Evolution of Bank-Industry Networks in Sweden and France", *Scandinavian Economic History Review*, 45, 244-256.

Marmefelt, Thomas, (1998), "Schumpeterian Banker-Entrepreneur Interaction and the Spontaneous Evolution of Bank-Industry Networks: Why Institutional Endowments Matter", in Klaus Nielsen and Björn Johnson (eds.), *Institutions and Economic Change: New Perspectives on Markets, Firms, and Technology*, Cheltenham: Edward Elgar.

Mayer, Colin, (1988), "New Issues in Corporate Finance", *European Economic Review*, 32, 1167-1189.

Mayer, Colin, (1990), "Financial Systems, Corporate Finance, and Economic Development", in R. Glenn Hubbard (ed.), *Asymmetric Information, Corporate Finance, and Investment*, Chicago: University of Chicago Press.

Mayer, Colin, and Ian Alexander, (1990), *Banks and Securities Markets: Corporate Financing in Germany and the UK*, CEPR Discussion Paper, No. 433.

McCauley, Robert N., and Steven A. Zimmer, (1989), "Explaining International

Differences in the Cost of Capital", *Federal Reserve Bank of New York Quarterly Review*, 14, 7-28.

Minsky, Hyman, (1990), "Schumpeter: Finance and Evolution", in Arnold Heertje and Mark Perlman (eds.), *Evolving Technology and Market Structure: Studies in Schumpeterian Economics*, Ann Arbor, MI: University of Michigan Press.

Mizruchi, Mark S., and Linda Brewster Stearns, (1994), "Money, Banking, and Financial Markets", in Neil J. Smelser and Richard Swedberg (eds.), *The Handbook of Economic Sociology*, Princeton, NJ: Princeton University Press.

Muldur, Ugur, (1990), "Restructurations et stratégies dans le secteur financier européen", *Revue d'Economie Financière*, No.12-13, 155-193.

Myers, Stewart C., (1984), "The Capital Structure Puzzle", *Journal of Finance*, 39, 572-592.

Nelson, Richard, and Sidney Winter, (1982), *An Evolutionary Theory of Economic Change*, Cambridge, MA: Belknap Press.

Nilsson, Göran B., (1981), *Banker i brytningstid: A O Wallenberg i svensk bank-politik 1850-56*, Stockholm: EHF.

Nygren, Ingemar, (1983), "Transformation of Bank Structures in the Industrial Period: The Case of Sweden 1820-1913", *Journal of European Economic History*, 12, 29-68.

OECD, (1985), *Trends in Banking in OECD Countries*, Paris.

OECD, (1986), *Banks and Specialised Financial Intermediaries in Development* (by Phillip Wellons, Dimitri Germidis, and Bianca Glavanis), Paris.

OECD, (1987a), *Asset and Liability Management by Banks* (by R. Harrington), Paris.

OECD, (1987b), *Structural Adjustment and Economic Performance*, Paris.

OECD, (1989a), *Competition in Banking* (by G.Bröker), Paris.

OECD, (1989b), *Economies in Transition: Structural Adjustment in OECD Countries*, Paris.

OECD, (1989c), *Evolution des structures, des besoins et des sources d'investissement industriel. L'investissement industriel dans une économie financière*, Paris.

OECD, (1992), *Banks under Stress*, Paris.

OECD, (1995), *National Systems for Financing Innovations*, Paris.

Olson, Mancur, (1965), *The Logic of Collective Action*, Cambridge, MA: Harvard University Press.

Pastré, Olivier, (1986), "La modernisation des relations entre les banques et les entreprises", *Revue d'Economie Industrielle*, No.35, 1st quarter, 213-224.

Pastré, Olivier, (1992), *Les nouveaux piliers de la finance*, Paris: La Découverte.

Patat, Jean-Pierre, (1987), *Monnaie, institutions financières et politique monétaire*, 4th ed, Paris: Economica.

Pelikan, Pavel, (1989), "Evolution, Economic Competence, and the Market for

Corporate Control", *Journal of Economic Behavior and Organization*, 12, 279-303, reprinted in Richard H. Day, Gunnar Eliasson, and Clas Wihlborg (eds.), (1993), *The Markets for Innovation, Ownership, and Control*, Amsterdam/London/New York/Tokyo: North-Holland.

Perez, Carlota, (1983), "Structural Change and the Assimilation of New Technologies in the Economic and Social Systems", *Futures*, 15, 357-375.

Plessis, Alain, (1987), "Le «retard français»: la faute à la banque? Banques locales, succursales de la Banque de France et financement de l'économie sous le second Empire", in Patrick Fridenson and André Straus (eds.), *Le capitalisme français-19e-20e siècle. Blocages et dynamismes d'une croissance*, Paris: Fayard.

Polanyi, Michael, (1967), *The Tacit Dimension*, London: Routledge.

Porter, Michael E., (1992), *Capital Choices: Changing the Way America Invests in Industry*, Washington DC: Council on Competitiveness.

Radner, Roy, (1992), "Hierarchy: The Economics of Managing", *Journal of Economic Literature*, 30, 1382-1415.

Rivaud-Danset, Dorothée, and Robert Salais, (1992), "Les conventions de financement des entreprises. Premières approches théorique et empirique, *Revue française d'économie*, 7:4, 81-120.

Saint-Paul, Gilles, (1992), "Technological Choice, Financial Markets, and Economic Development", *European Economic Review*, 36, 763-781.

Salter, W.E.G., (1960), *Productivity and Technical Change*, Cambridge: Cambridge University Press.

Sandberg, Lars G., (1978), "Banking and Economic Growth in Sweden before World War I", *Journal of Economic History*, 38, 650-680.

Sandberg, Lars G., (1979), "The Case of the Impoverished Sophisticate: Human Capital and Swedish Economic Growth before World War I", *Journal of Economic History*, 39, 225-241.

Sandler, Todd, (1992), *Collective Action: Theory and Applications*, Ann Arbor, MI: University of Michigan Press.

Santarelli, Enrico, (1989), "Financial and Technological Innovations during the Phases of Capitalist Development", in Massimo Di Matteo, Richard M. Goodwin, and Alessandro Vercelli (eds.), *Technological and Social Factors in Long Term Fluctuations*, Berlin: Springer-Verlag.

Schotter, Andrew, (1981), *The Economic Theory of Social Institutions*, Cambridge: Cambridge University Press.

Schumpeter, Joseph A., (1911), *Theorie der wirtschaftlichen Entwicklung: Eine Untersuchung über Unternehmengewinn, Kapital, Kredit, Zins und den Konjunkturzyklus*, 4th ed, Munich/Leipzig: Duncker & Humblot, 1935.

Schumpeter, Joseph A., (1939), *Business Cycles: A Theoretical, Historical, and Statistical Analysis of the Capitalist Process*, New York/London: McGraw-

Hill.

Schumpeter, Joseph A., (1942), *Capitalism, Socialism, and Democracy*, New York/London: Harper & Brothers.

Schön, Lennart, (1994), *Omvandling och obalans: Mönster i svensk ekonomisk utveckling*, Bilaga 3 till Långtidsutredningen 1994, Stockholm: Ministry of Finance.

Segerstrom, Paul S., T.C.A. Anant, and Elias Dinopoulos, (1990), "A Schumpeterian Model of the Product Life Cycle", *American Economic Review*, 80, 1077-1091.

Sejersted, Francis, (1988), "Bank og samfunn: Forretningsbankenes forhold til næringslivet", *Bergen Bank Kvartalsskrift*, 22:4, 95-103.

Sharpe, Steven A., (1990), "Asymmetric Information, Bank Lending, and Implicit Contracts: A Stylized Model of Customer Relationships", *Journal of Finance*, 45, 1069-1087.

Simon, Herbert, (1959), "Theories of Decision-Making in Economics and Behavioral Science", *American Economic Review*, 49, 253-283.

Steinherr, Alfred, and Christian Huveneers, (1990), *Universal Banks: The Prototype of Successful Banks in the Integrated European Market?: A View Inspired by the German Experience*, CEPS Research Report No.2, Brussels.

Stiglitz, Joseph E., and Andrew Weiss, (1981), "Credit Rationing in Markets with Imperfect Information", *American Economic Review*, 71, 393-410.

Streissler, Erich, (1982), Schumpeter's Vienna and the Role of Credit in Innovation", in H. Frisch (ed.), *Schumpeterian Economics*, New York: Praeger Publishers.

Sugden, Robert, (1986), *The Economics of Rights, Cooperation, and Welfare*, Oxford: Basil Blackwell.

Sugden, Robert, (1991), "Rational Choice: A Survey of Contributions from Economics and Philosophy", *Economic Journal*, 101, 751-785.

Sveriges Riksbank, (1991), *Kredit- och Valutamarknaden 1990*, Stockholm.

Talele, Chaitram, (1988), "Schumpeterian Financing of Economic Development", *Indian Economic Journal*, 35, 72-85.

Teubal, Morris, and Ehud Zuscovitch, (1994), "Demand Revealing and Knowledge Differentiation Through Network Evolution", in Börje Johansson, Charlie Karlsson, and Lars Westin (eds.), *Patterns of a Network Economy*, Berlin/Heidelberg: Springer-Verlag.

Thunholm, Lars-Erik, (1989), *Svenskt kreditväsen*, 11th revised edition, Stockholm: Rabén&Sjögren.

Tilly, Richard, (1986), "Financing Industrial Enterprise in Great Britain and Germany in the Nineteenth Century: Testing Grounds for Marxist and Schumpeterian Theories?", in H.-J. Wagener and J. W. Drukker (eds.), *The Economic Law of Motion of Modern Society: A Marx-Keynes-Schumpeter Centen-*

nial, Cambridge: Cambridge University Press.

Tobin, James, (1984), "On the Efficiency of the Financial System", *Lloyds Bank Review*, 153, 1-15.

Ullmann-Margalit, Edna, (1977), *The Emergence of Norms*, Oxford: Clarendon Press.

Vercelli, Alessandro, (1989), "Uncertainty, Technological Flexibility, and Long Term Fluctuations", in Massimo Di Matteo, Richard M. Goodwin, and Alessandro Vercelli (eds.), *Technological and Social Factors in Long Term Fluctuations*, Berlin: Springer-Verlag.

Viñals, José, and Angel Berges, (1988), "Financial Innovation and Capital Formation", in Arnold Heertje (ed.), *Innovation, Technology, and Finance*, Oxford: Basil Blackwell.

von Neumann, John, (1945), "A Model of General Equilibrium", *Review of Economic Studies*, 13, 1-9.

Whitley, Richard, (1990), "East Asian Enterprise Structures and the Comparative Analysis of Business Organizations", *Organization Studies*, 11, 47-74.

Whitley, Richard, (1992), "Societies, Firms, and Markets: The Social Structuring of Business Systems", in Richard Whitley (ed.), *Firms and Markets in their National Contexts*, London: Sage.

Wicksell, Knut, (1898), *Geldzins und Güterpreise*, Jena: G.Fischer.

Wicksell, Knut, (1906), *Föreläsningar i nationalekonomi*, Lund: Berlingska.

Witt, Ulrich, (1986), "Evolution and Stability of Cooperation without Enforceable Contracts", *Kyklos*, 39, 245-266.

Witt, Ulrich, (1989), "The Evolution of Economic Institutions as a Propagation Process", *Public Choice*, 62, 155-172.

Witt, Ulrich, (1996a), "A 'Darwinian Revolution' in Economics?", *Journal of Institutional and Theoretical Economics*, 152, 707-715.

Witt, Ulrich, (1996b), "Innovations, Externalities and the Problem of Economic Progress", *Public Choice*, 89, 113-130.

Witt, Ulrich, (1997), *'Lock-In' vs. 'Critical Masses' - Industrial Change under Network Externalities*, Papers on Economics & Evolution, No. 9701, Jena: Max-Planck-Institute for Research into Economc Systems.

Yakushiji, Taizo, (1984), "Reshuffling Firms for Technology?: An Aggregate Time Series Analysis of B. Klein's Dynamic Efficiency", in Masahiko Aoki (ed.), *The Economic Analysis of the Japanese Firm*, Amsterdam: North-Holland.

Zimmer, Steven A., and Robert N. McCauley, (1991), "Bank Cost of Capital and International Competition", *Federal Reserve Bank of New York Quarterly Review*, 15, 33-59.

Zysman, John, (1983), *Governments, Markets, and Growth: Financial Systems and the Politics of Industrial Change*, Oxford: Martin Robertson.

Index